Monte

Hope you enjoy this photo/info record!
I know the beginning pictures well! My
Dad, brother Jim & I found a huge
piece of jade just down from the C.P.R
bridge!

Merry Christmas and
Great Travel Plans for
the New Year!

"Uncle" Neal

# WESTERN CANADA'S

# RAILWAYS

The **Canadian**, behind VIA RAIL's 1414, bursts from the west portal of the Connaught Tunnel, on the CPR mainline through the Rogers Pass.

# WESTERN CANADA'S

# RAILWAYS

by

## J. Edward Martin

## STUDIO E

**British Columbia, Canada.**

**Canadian Cataloguing in Publication Data**

```
Martin, J. Edward.
  Western Canada's railways



     Bibliography: p.
     Includes index.
     ISBN 0-920716-01-6

     1. Railroads - Canada, Western - History.*
I. Title.
HE2808.M37 1986       385'.09712      C86-091461-5
```

Number _653_
Of A Limited Edition
Of _1000_ Copies

Distributed by

**J.E. MARTIN**
**306—1360 FIR STREET**
**WHITE ROCK, B.C.**
**CANADA   V4B 4B2**

Printed in Canada

ISBN 0-920716-01-6

# CONTENTS

Preface . . . . . . . . . . . . . . . . . . . . . . . . . . . . . . . . . . . . . . . . . . . . . . . . . . 7

**TRANSCONTINENTALS**

Canadian Pacific Railway . . . . . . . . . . . . . . . . . . . . . . . . . . . . . . . 9
— Esquimalt & Nanaimo Rwy . . . . . . . . . . . . . . . . . . . . . . . . . . 23
Canadian National Railways . . . . . . . . . . . . . . . . . . . . . . . . . . . 29
— Great Slave Lake Rwy . . . . . . . . . . . . . . . . . . . . . . . . . . . . . . 42
— Alberta Resources Rwy . . . . . . . . . . . . . . . . . . . . . . . . . . . . . 42
— Northern Alberta Railways . . . . . . . . . . . . . . . . . . . . . . . . . . 43
Burlington Northern Railroad . . . . . . . . . . . . . . . . . . . . . . . . . . 47

**COLOR SECTION** . . . . . . . . . . . . . . . . . . . . . . . . . . . . . . . . . 49

**REGIONALS**

British Columbia Railway . . . . . . . . . . . . . . . . . . . . . . . . . . . . . . 57
B.C. Hydro Railway . . . . . . . . . . . . . . . . . . . . . . . . . . . . . . . . . . 66
White Pass & Yukon Route . . . . . . . . . . . . . . . . . . . . . . . . . . . . 76

**INDUSTRIALS**

Greater Winnipeg Water District Rwy . . . . . . . . . . . . . . . . . . . . 85
Logging Lines . . . . . . . . . . . . . . . . . . . . . . . . . . . . . . . . . . . . . . . 89
Canadian Forest Products Railway . . . . . . . . . . . . . . . . . . . . . . 91
Crown Forest Industries Railway . . . . . . . . . . . . . . . . . . . . . . . . 95
Other Industrials . . . . . . . . . . . . . . . . . . . . . . . . . . . . . . . . . . . . 99

**RAPID TRANSIT**

Introduction . . . . . . . . . . . . . . . . . . . . . . . . . . . . . . . . . . . . . . . . 103
Edmonton LRT . . . . . . . . . . . . . . . . . . . . . . . . . . . . . . . . . . . . . 109
Calgary LRT . . . . . . . . . . . . . . . . . . . . . . . . . . . . . . . . . . . . . . . 112
Vancouver Regional ALRT . . . . . . . . . . . . . . . . . . . . . . . . . . . . 115

**INDEX** . . . . . . . . . . . . . . . . . . . . . . . . . . . . . . . . . . . . . . . . . . 118

**BIBLIOGRAPHY** . . . . . . . . . . . . . . . . . . . . . . . . . . . . . . . . . . 120

Lethbridge viaduct, on the CPR Crow's Nest line in southern Alberta. At a dizzying 314 feet above the Belly River, it is the highest railway bridge in Canada. It is also one of the longest: 5,327 feet, and requires 33 steel towers to support it. It was opened in October, 1909.

## PICTURE CREDITS

# PREFACE

*There is perhaps little hint in to-day's mile upon mile of grain fields, numerous brightly lit cities and bustling ports, that hardly more than a century ago the Canadian West was nearly total wilderness. Coyotes are still free to howl at trains in the night but nature as a whole has been well and truly harnessed. The bisons that once roamed the prairies by the millions, the decorated Indian tipis, the totem poles and the trading posts have all become museum curiosities, while the land has been transformed into one of the world's greatest sources of food, wood and minerals.*

*At the base of this great change in landscape, economy and population were the railways, for the requisite massive influx of settlers, machinery and materials and corresponding outflow of grain, lumber and ore, were possible in no other way. No deep water routes penetrate the West's interior and the roundabout system of rivers, lakes and portages used by the voyageurs of earlier times would have been hopelessly inadequate. Hindering overland access from the East were a thousand miles of brush and muskeg in northern Ontario, while travel inland from the west coast was blocked by chain after chain of north to south mountains, land so difficult to traverse it remained largely unexplored until after 1850.*

*The extent of the railways' accomplishments becomes all the more impressive when one considers the many other natural problems they have faced. The dry summers encourage tremendous grass and forest fires. Grasshoppers and caterpillars occasionally become so numerous that their crushed bodies on the rails bring trains to a slithering halt. Water in places can be so alkaline as to be unfit for drinking and its tendency to foam profusely when heated made it useless for steam locomotives.*

*In the mountains, unstable rock threatens instant disaster. At Frank, Alberta in 1903, it took less than two minutes for the town, its inhabitants and rail line to be buried beneath 45 feet of stone. Boulders the size of boxcars still occasionally land on rails through the Rockies and avalanches are a yearly menace. Even more widespread, however, is the intense winter cold, which freezes hands and turnouts, cracks rails and loosens airbrake gaskets on lines throughout the West.*

*About the only thing Canadian railways were more or less spared were attacks by Indians and train robbers. While the Americans experienced a great deal of violence, there were no pitched battles between railwaymen and redskins on this side of the border. And whereas the United States witnessed 59 train holdups between 1870 and 1933, Canada had only four, the first of which did not occur until 10 September 1904, when Bill Miner, an American, robbed a train at gunpoint near Mission, B.C.*

*As the Canadian West matured, its railways changed as well. The old colonist coaches, with their hard wooden benches and small stoves used by countless immigrants and harvest workers, are now only memories. Gone too are the silk trains that sped the valuable oriental fabric across the continent faster than the best expresses. And the horse train, that uniquely Canadian phenomenon that saw race animals and their owners move in style from Calgary to all the major fairs, has likewise become a thing of the past, like many things a victim of the growth of highways.*

*Since the Second World War, more and more section houses and small stations have been lost in the drive for centralization but the most profound change, and the one most bitterly regretted by railfans, was the replacement of steam power with diesels. The sound*

7

and smell of railways has never been the same, water towers and roundhouses have all but vanished, trains have become longer, and crews have diminished in both size and number since that lamentable time.

In the following pages, the fascinating variety and the growing size of equipment will at once be apparent. Foreign readers will no doubt remark upon the lack of progress in electrification and passenger train technology but they will also note the winds of change evident in the building of BC Rail's Tumbler Ridge line and the relatively recent construction of three fine, new rapid transit systems. It should be clear as well that while the number of railways continues to decline and fall into government ownership, the improvements to those that remain are indeed extensive. The prosperity and well-being of the western provinces has in the past depended heavily upon steel rails and it is highly improbable that there will be any great change in that situation for a very long time to come.

Canadian Pacific number 374, the historic locomotive that ushered in a new era for Vancouver when it arrived with the first passenger train, on 23 May 1887. It is shown here in Kitsilano Park, several years before it was removed for display in front of the old CPR roundhouse at Expo 86.

# CANADIAN PACIFIC

In a little over a hundred years the Canadian Pacific, Canada's first transcontinental railway, has grown into a huge corporation with interests in hotels, real estate, mining and refining, flour milling, forest products, petroleum and telecommunications. Its ships travel the globe and its influence on world trade has reached monumental proportions.

Western lines of the railway are divided into two parts. The Prairie Region, over 5,500 miles of track in all, extends from Thunder Bay, Ontario to Swift Current, Saskatchewan, while the 4,750 mile Pacific Region continues west to Port Alberni, on Vancouver Island. Head offices are located in Montreal but western operations are largely handled from important regional headquarters in Vancouver, Calgary and Winnipeg.

Considerable increases in bulk commodity shipments (mainly coal, grain, sulphur and potash) have heavily burdened western lines in recent years. Sixty million tons of freight were travelling annually over the British Columbia mainline alone by the 1980s and double tracking became a priority over much of the system. Portions that had been taken up when Central Traffic Control was introduced in the 1950s had to be relaid and six hundred million dollars were allocated to building new tunnels in the Rogers Pass.

CP Rail is a dynamic, sophisticated system that does not hesitate to employ the latest technology. Lasers are used to accurately align track. Satellites relay messages from dispatchers to train crews in the Rockies and computers handle a plethora of data concerning equipment and car movement. Microprocessors monitor progress of trains in certain areas, while helicopters patrol wilderness regions regulating problems caused by beaver dams and forest fires.

Until the 1950s, passenger service received considerable attention on the railway. Vacations at the chateau-styled Banff and Lake Louise hotels were heavily promoted, along with daylight service through the scenic Rockies in trains equipped with observation coaches. Handsome engines caught the public's eye and freights were obliged to scurry for the nearest siding when a "varnish" was due. Unfortunately, all these things changed as air and road competition intensified and by the 1960s the railway was eager to drop its passenger operations altogether. It was more than relieved in 1977, when the federal government created VIA RAIL corporation to take over the ailing and unprofitable service.

Modern CP Rail freight trains now rule the rails and are an impressive sight to behold. Their average length is about a hundred cars and in the Rogers Pass as many as twelve locomotives have been needed to move them, with units placed at front, middle and rear. On the Prairie Region, trains can be even longer and it was there that a record-setting 252 car grain train was run in 1974, from Winnipeg to Thunder Bay. The nearly 20,000 ton load stretched for two and a half miles (four kilometres) and had to be broken into four parts before it could enter the yards.

Whenever possible, freight is grouped into solid trains of the same commodity. For some items, such as coal, unit trains of identical cars have been devised. They move back and forth between mine and port in an endless procession, rarely needing to be uncoupled. Efficiency is improved by both types of train, as sorting is reduced, if not eliminated, and the number of loads per car per year is substantially increased.

Traffic on the CPR generally moves in an east-west pattern but the company has important links with American railroads. It acquired a controlling interest in the Minneapolis, St. Paul & Sault Ste. Marie Railway (now known as the Soo Line) as far back as 1888. In the great days of passenger service, twenty-three coach excursion trains could be found running from Chicago through Moose Jaw to Banff. Daily flyers connected Spokane with Chicago via Kingsgate, Lethbridge, Moose Jaw, etc. in the early part of the century and regular Soo Line trains ran to Winnipeg from various U.S. points. The Soo Line, basically a grain carrier, has in more recent years prospered carrying Canadian potash and sulphur to American markets and its usefulness was further enhanced by the 1985 takeover of the Milwaukee Road, whose lines extended south to Kansas City and Louisville.

By a twist of fate, the Canadian Pacific narrowly missed being tightly enmeshed with the Burlington Northern Railroad. The same syndicate involved in the building of the CPR also headed the St. Paul & Pacific Railway, later the Great Northern and eventually the BNR. In 1878, Donald Smith, his cousin George Stephen and James J. Hill bought the St. P&P and it soon became connected to the embryo of the CPR, the Pembina Branch Railway, that ran south from Winnipeg to the border, at Emerson. It was not until 1884, only a year before the last spike on the Canadian Pacific was driven, that Hill withdrew from the CPR syndicate over building an all-Canadian route around the north shore of Lake Superior. Had Hill stayed, the history of the company would no doubt have been much different. Hill wanted to divert traffic entirely southward to U.S. plants. It was he that hired Major A. B. Rogers, an American engineer, to find a pass through the Rockies well to the south of the Yellowhead, which had been chosen earlier by Sandford Fleming. It was also Hill that appointed William C. Van Horne, another American, to the general managership of the CPR in 1882 but there he must have been disappointed, for Van Horne saw to it that the Canadian Pacific won the race with the Great Northern to the coast and effectively blocked GN incursions into Canada. The CP's Crow's Nest line through Lethbridge to the Kootenays in 1898 gradually reversed Great Northern growth on this side of the border and the CPR grew to dominate the entire southern portion of the western provinces. The Kootenay & Elk Railway scheme of the early 1970s, which would have drained coal traffic once again south to Burlington Northern lines, has been about the only threat to that dominance in recent times.

The wonder of the CPR is that it is and has been since its inception, a private enterprise. The federal government had surveys and even some construction done on it prior to incorporation, for it was a national project, a necessity both for the entry of British Columbia into Confederation and for the retention of Canadian sovereignty in the West. The Americans had completed their first transcontinental railroad, the Union Pacific, in May 1869 and the Northern Pacific, running only a short distance south of the Canadian border, was begun the next year. Although the 49th parallel had been established as the western Canadian-U.S. frontier, the memory of the American takeover of thinly-settled Mexican Texas, California and the southwest territories in the 1840s was still vivid. How the Canadian Pacific could then have been conceived, born, encouraged to grow and then thrive for over a hundred years on its own, especially in light of the fact that a national railway had developed apart in the interim, is clearly something of a mystery.

It would be inappropriate to detail the long and involved history of the Canadian Pacific Railway here but a bibliography of recommended books on the subject is provided on the last page of this volume, in addition to the following chronology.

# CPR CHRONOLOGY for Western Lines

1867 — Confederation of eastern Canadian provinces, 1 July.

1871 — British Columbia enters Confederation on condition a transcontinental railway is built.
     — Sandford Fleming surveys a route through the Yellowhead Pass.

1878 — Pembina Branch Rwy. (St. Boniface to Pembina/Emerson) opens in November and connects with the St. Paul & Pacific Rwy.

1880 — Construction begins at Yale, B.C. eastward, 15 May, under government sponsorship.

1881 — Incorporation of the Canadian Pacific Railway Co., 15 February.

1882 — Construction westward across the prairies begins in Spring, from Winnipeg.
     — Port Arthur (now Thunder Bay) to Winnipeg section completed, 19 June.
     — Major Rogers announces discovery of a new pass through the Selkirks in August.

1883 — First train reaches Calgary on August 10th.

1884 — James J. Hill withdraws from the CPR syndicate.

1885 — Second North West Rebellion, under Louis Riel, demonstrates need for completion of the CPR.
     — Last spike driven at Craigellachie, in Eagle Pass, B.C., 7 November.

1886 — First scheduled transcontinental train arrives in Port Moody, B.C. on July 4th.

1888 — Van Horne succeeds George Stephen as president of the CPR.

1891 — Calgary & Edmonton Rwy. built (Macleod to Strathcona).
     — Shuswap & Okanagan Rwy. built (Sicamous to Okanagan Landing, B.C.).
     — Mission to Huntingdon, B.C. branch (for a Northern Pacific interchange) completed in May.

1897 — CPR agrees to build a Lethbridge-Nelson line and accepts fixed rate on grain shipment to the lakehead in exchange for land grants and construction subsidies.

1898 — Columbia & Western Rwy. and smelter at Trail, B.C. leased in perpetuity.

1899 — Crow's Nest Pass line (Lethbridge-Kootenay Landing) opened, 18 June.

1900 — Manitoba North Western Rwy. (Portage la Prairie-Yorkton) acquired.

1902 — Vancouver & Lulu Island Rwy. built by CPR Vancouver-Steveston.

1905 — V&LI Rwy. leased to the BCER.

1909 — Spiral tunnels, between Hector and Field, B.C. are built.
     — Lethbridge viaduct, highest railway bridge in Canada, completed in October.

1912 — Esquimalt & Nanaimo Railway, on Vancouver Island, leased.

1914 — Kootenay Central Rwy. (Golden south to Crow's Nest line) completed.

1916 — Kettle Valley route (Nelson to Hope via Coquihalla canyon) completed.
     — Connaught Tunnel eliminates over-the-Rogers Pass route, 9 December.

1937 — First diesel-electric locomotive, switcher No. 7000, delivered by National Steel Car Corp.

1959 — Storm damage leads to abandonment of the Coquihalla line.

1960 — Last steam engine, No. 29, operates (Montreal-St. Lin special).

1961 — The Minneapolis, St. Paul & Sault Ste. Marie, the Duluth, South Shore & Atlantic and the Wisconsin Central railways merge into the Soo Line Railroad Co.

1968 — Name CP Rail replaces Canadian Pacific Railway Co.

1970 — First unit coal train reaches Roberts Bank April 30th.

1978 — VIA RAIL takes over CPR passenger service, 29 September.

1979 — Penticton to Midway line in B.C. closed.

1984 — Crow Rates abolished, 1 January.
     — New tunnel project in the Rogers Pass is begun.

1986 — V&LI lines returned to CPR after lease expires.

Two of the many CPR emblems that featured the industrious beaver.

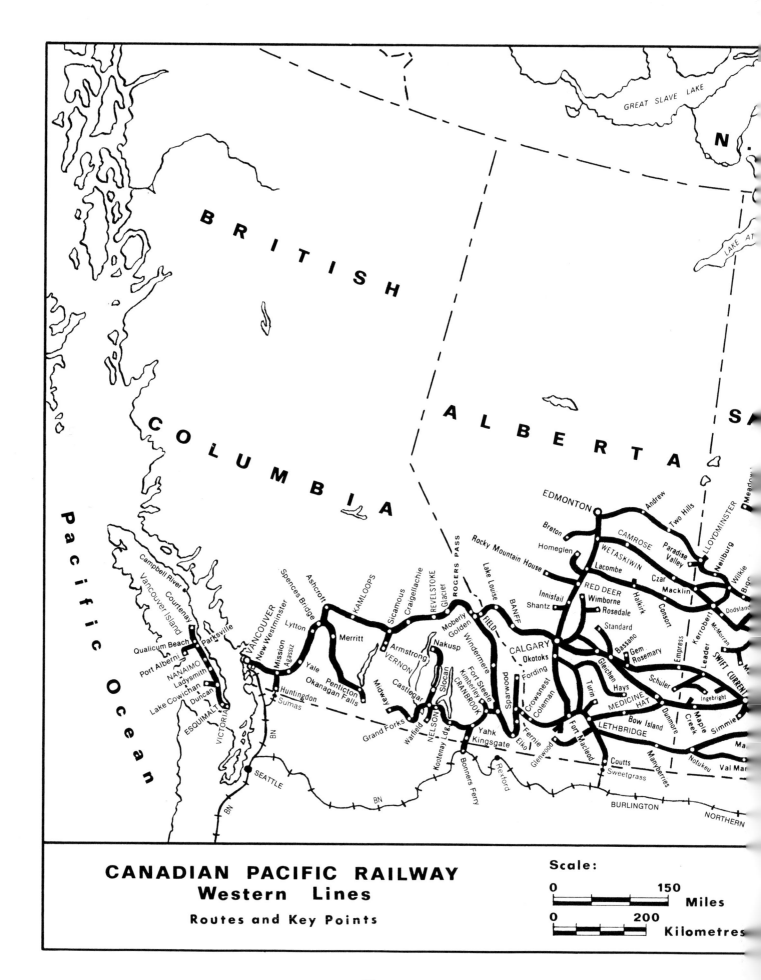

# CANADIAN PACIFIC RAILWAY
## Western Lines
### Routes and Key Points

Scale:

0 — 150 Miles

0 — 200 Kilometres

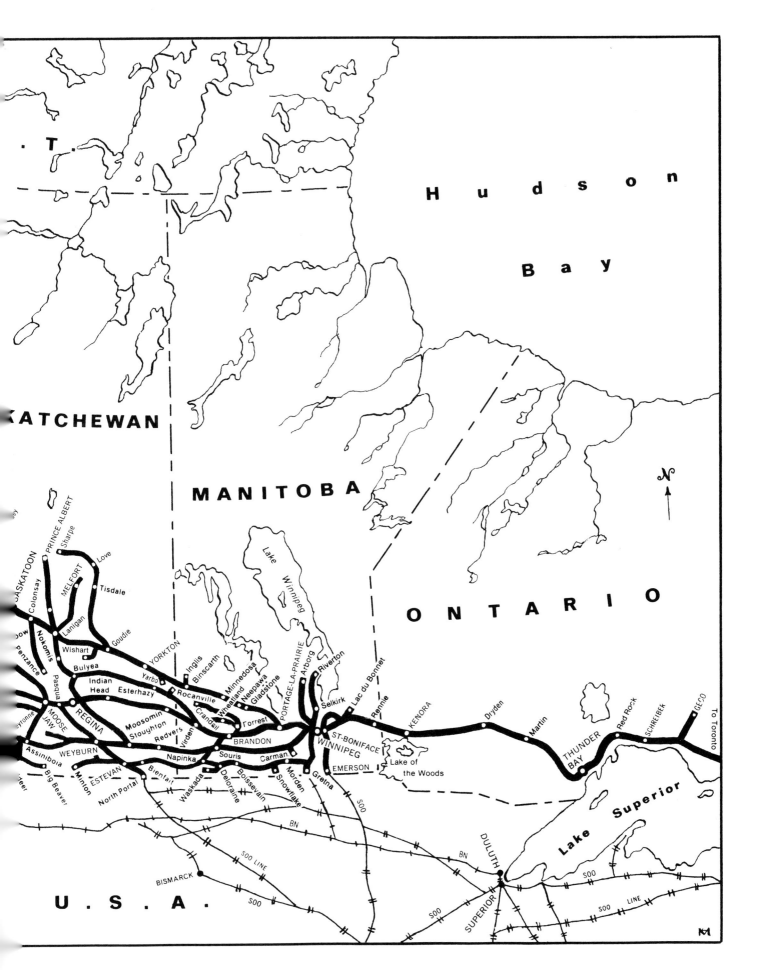

N.W.T.

KATCHEWAN

MANITOBA

ONTARIO

Hudson Bay

PRINCE ALBERT
Sharpe
Love
MELFORT
Tisdale
SASKATOON
Colonsay
Lanigan
Goudie
Wishart
YORKTON
Bulyea
Inglis
Binscarth
Nokomis
Pasqua
Indian Head
Esterhazy
Rocanville
Minnedosa
Neepawa
Gladstone
Yarbo
Wheatland
Crandell
Forrest
PORTAGE-LA-PRAIRIE
Arborg
Riverton
penzance
REGINA
Moosomin
Stoughton
Redvers
Virden
BRANDON
Selkirk
Lac du Bonnet
MOOSE JAW
Souris
Carman
WINNIPEG
ST-BONIFACE
Rennie
KENORA
Dryden
Martin
THUNDER BAY
Red Rock
SCHREIBER
GECO
To Toronto
eyonne
Napinka
WEYBURN
Assiniboia
Minton
Bienfait
Waskada
Deloraine
Boissevain
Snowflake
Morden
Gretna
EMERSON
Lake of the Woods
Big Beaver
ESTEVAN
North Portal
eer
BISMARCK
SOO LINE
BN
SOO
BN
DULUTH
SUPERIOR
SOO
SOO LINE
Lake Superior

U. S. A.

SOO

13

Tunnels in the Rogers and Kicking Horse passes did not remove the need for better, more powerful locomotives between Calgary and Revelstoke. Loads and equipment were becoming steadily heavier as the years passed. Average weight of a passenger train in 1918, for instance, was 375 tons. By 1930, it had reached 512. Meeting demands best in the Rockies were the 2-10-4 Selkirk class engines, built between 1929 and 1949. Number 5901, shown above, was one of the first. Packing 89,000 pounds tractive effort (including booster) and weighing 453,000 lbs., it was the strongest and heaviest steam locomotive in the country.

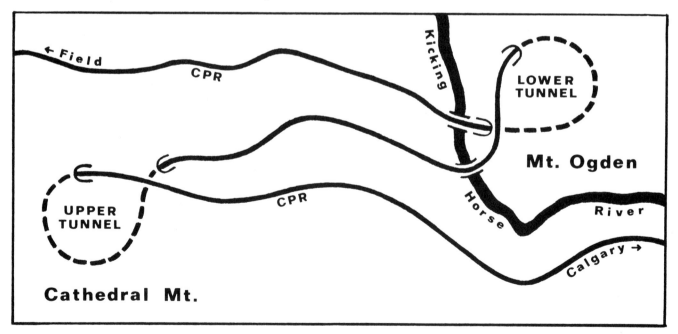

The Spiral Tunnels, built to overcome the hazards and costs of the "Big Hill" in the Kicking Horse Pass, east of Field, B.C., reduced the ruling grade from 4.5 per cent to a more manageable 2.2. Opened in September 1909, they remain unique in North American railroading.

Highway trailers, piggyback on flatcars, moving through snow sheds in the Rogers Pass area. Before the Connaught Tunnel was built in 1913-16, the over-the-summit route had over 30 such sheds, a couple over a mile long. Even these were not enough to prevent avalanches from claiming seven lives at the Rogers Pass station in January, 1899, nor another 62 at the summit in March, 1910.

Wedge type snowplows (RIGHT) usually manage to keep rail lines open through the Rockies but when slides occur, or when storms dump too much of the white stuff at once, bulldozers have to be brought in. Howitzers to bring down menacing snow build-ups and electric detector fences to warn of blockages on the line are among other modern devices used in the yearly battle with the Canadian winter.

TOP LEFT: Excavated material from the Mount Macdonald tunnel leaving in a mining train. Situated 109 metres below the old Connaught tunnel, and with a maximum gradient of only 1%, the new tunnel was designed to carry the westbound, heaviest trains. Eastbound traffic would continue to use the older, steeper line, effecting a double track route. The Connaught lost its double tracking in 1958, when higher freight cars, notably auto racks, came into use.

LEFT: A huge, 302 tonne tunnel boring machine, or "mole", used on the East heading of the Mount Macdonald tunnel. Its 6.8 metre (22.3 foot) diameter cutting head excavated no less than 62.78 metres of rock in a 24 hour period in April, 1986, a world record. The 14.66 km (9.1 mile) length of the completed tunnel is also a record for North America. A 1.82 km (1.1 mile) tunnel beneath Mount Shaughnessy, six bridges and ten miles of surface work were also involved in this giant Rogers Pass project of 1984-88.

LOWER LEFT: Hot box detector, east of Vancouver, for monitoring passing train axles. It signals the position of any bearings that are abnormally hot, using the light panel above. Even more sophisticated detectors, with synthesized voices, were placed in service on the CPR Prairie Region in 1985.

A classic scene from the classic era of passenger train service: a semi-streamlined Selkirk at work amid the scenic grandeur of Banff, Alberta, about 1939.

Semi-streamlined Hudson 4-6-4s built for the company by Montreal Locomotive Works starting in 1937, easily handled the long, heavy Thunder Bay-Winnipeg, Winnipeg-Calgary and Revelstoke-Vancouver assignments. The crown on the running board of 2860 at right, shown in excursion service on the BCR in the 1980s, commemorates sister engine 2850's hauling of the Royal Train from Quebec City to Vancouver, in 1939.

First of the CPR streamliners and Canada's fastest, with an official speed record of 112.5 mph set by engine 3003 in 1936, were the Jubilees. Number 3001 (ABOVE) pulled the lightweight-coached **Chinook** on the Edmonton-Calgary run before being scrapped in 1957. Several later models provided similar high-speed service elsewhere on the prairies before dieselization.

Typical of the sober, classical railway architecture of the early 20th century was the styling of Fort William's Union Station (BELOW), built in 1910 for the CPR and the Grand Trunk Pacific.

On 24 April 1955, the gleaming, stainless steel **Canadian** began its famous Transcontinental service. Above, it stops at Kenora, Ontario in the Spring of 1971. On the tail board of its glass-domed observation coach is the geometric CP Rail logo introduced three years earlier.

Open observation coaches similar to the one shown on page 60 were introduced on the CPR as early as 1890, for use in the magnificent Rockies. In 1902, glass booths were placed on some models but none of the early cars offered the comfort of the airconditioned vista dome of the **Canadian,** shown at right. These continued to be used by VIA through the 1980s.

Canadian Pacific's Nelson, B.C. installation. Divisional offices for the Kootenays are located in the large frame station of 1900, seen at centre right.

LEFT: A CPR rotary plow, pushed by a 4-6-0 leaves Lethbridge, Alberta for the Crow's Nest Pass, about 1912. Although capable of cutting through very deep snow, they were nevertheless abandoned occasionally in places like the Coquihalla area and were subject to hazards like hidden rock and timber carried onto the rails in avalanches - devastating to the rotating blades of the plow.

RIGHT: Continuous loading of a Canadian Pacific unit train at Byron Creek mine, in southeastern British Columbia. The gondola cars are in effect buckets on a conveyor system to Thunder Bay, where the coal is transferred to lake boats, for delivery to Ontario Hydro and other eastern customers.

BELOW: Another unit coal train from the Kootenays heads west on its 700 mile journey to Roberts Bank, south of Vancouver. The scene is the well known Stoney Creek steel arch bridge near the Rogers Pass.

End of the line for some CP Rail grain traffic: the Alberta Wheat Pool terminal elevator in Vancouver. Grain passes by conveyor into the concrete silos, where it is cleaned, treated and stored before being loaded onto ships at the rear.

LEFT: An eastbound train moves over the Louise Bridge, bound for Thunder Bay. The structure was built over the Red River by the City of Winnipeg in 1881 to ensure that the railway expanded westward from there, rather than from the town of Selkirk, to the North. The CPR was also given land for its station and right-of-way, which remained tax-free until 1965.

# ESQUIMALT & NANAIMO RAILWAY

Although the E&N Railway is operated as a division of CP Rail's Pacific Region (which extends from Swift Current, Saskatchewan to Port Alberni, B.C.) it has always maintained its own name and special identity. Its 200 odd miles of track in southeastern Vancouver Island have never experienced the huge tonnages and heavy usage seen on the CP's mainland operations, because grain is not a crop for the island and mining has almost disappeared. Most of the E&N's freight to-day is composed of forest products and passenger service has dwindled to a single train a day each way between Victoria and Courtenay.

The history of the E&N is of singular interest. Its inception lay in the confederation of British Columbia with Canada in 1871, an agreement that hinged upon a promise of a rail link to the eastern provinces. Subsequent surveys indicated that a direct rail line from Vancouver Island to the mainland would be excessively costly, so the western terminus of the proposed transcontinental railway was changed from Victoria to Burrard Inlet (the Vancouver area). Thus the E&N failed to begin its operating life as part of the CPR. Instead, it was an independent line owned by a small syndicate headed by two Scottish immigrants, Robert and James Dunsmuir, backed by American railroad tycoons Charles Crocker, Leland Stanford and Collis P. Huntington.

By 1884, work had begun on the railway and on August 13th, 1886 the last spike was driven at Cliffside, about 25 miles north of Victoria, by no less a personage than the Prime Minister of Canada, John A. Macdonald. The city of Victoria remained unconnected for another two years, because of the need for bridgework over the Inner Harbour.

The Dunsmuir family, heavily involved in coal mining on the island, decided to sell the E&N to the Canadian Pacific Railway in 1905. For various reasons, however, the E&N was not absorbed directly into the CPR. Rather, it was leased for a period of 999 years, starting in 1912. Documents and advertising continued to refer to the E&N as a distinct entity but except for a few boxcars with E&N initials within otherwise standard CP Rail decoration, the name disappeared from equipment.

The CPR planned much greater expansion of the E&N than was actually realized. Branches were built to Port Alberni and to Cowichan Lake in 1911 but lines beyond, to Comox Lake and to Long Beach halted at Great Central. The Campbell River extension stopped at Courtenay, well short of its intended destination.

Since undisturbed movement of certain freight is commonly necessary, rail car ferries have long connected the E&N to the mainland. A ferry slip was built at Ladysmith, south of Nanaimo in 1899 to serve both the E&N and the Wellington Colliery Railway (another Dunsmuir enterprise). A ferry terminal was also opened at Nanoose Bay, north of Wellington in 1921 but both of these facilities were later replaced by the Nanaimo slip, opened in 1953. Containers and trailers may move through Victoria or other ports on the island but the main rail connection point to-day remains Nanaimo.

In early years, regular passenger trains were well patronized and at the turn of the century some even carried luxurious parlor cars. All the branches were served by 1913 but with the advent of bus and automobile competition soon afterward, rail service went into a steady decline. An application to abandon passenger service altogether was made in the 1960s but permission was denied. Eventually, in 1978, the federal government's VIA Rail corporation took over passenger operations on the line. While it can not be denied that rides along it are indeed very pleasurable, with lush forest scenery punctuated by beautiful marine views, much more frequent service and new equipment would be needed to make it very useful for everyday purposes.

## E & N RAILWAY CHRONOLOGY

1871 — British Columbia joins Confederation.
1873 — Sod turned at Esquimalt in July.
1879 — Burrard Inlet replaces Victoria as western terminus of the transcontinental railway.
1881 — Charter granted Victoria, Esquimalt & Nanaimo Rwy.
1884 — Construction of the E&N begins.
1886 — Last spike driven at Cliffside August 13th.
1887 — Nanaimo to Wellington extension built.
1888 — Victoria connected March 28th.
1905 — E&N assets purchased by CPR June 8th.
1911 — Port Alberni branch opened December 20th.
       — Cowichan Lake branch built.
1912 — E&N leased to CPR.
1914 — Extension Parksville to Courtenay completed August 6th.
1925 — Port Alberni to Great Central branch opened.
1949 — Complete dieselization.
1978 — VIA takes over passenger service.

Esquimalt E&NR yards in the 1980s. The car repair shops at left, and parts of the roundhouse to the right, date back to the line's beginnings, over a century ago.

Locomotive number 2 on a timber trestle at Goldstream, a few miles north of Esquimalt, in 1885. Bridges were and are common on the E&N but only one tunnel, at mile 15.6, not far from this photo's location, was ever required.

The picturesque station at Qualicum Beach, built in 1914. Its picket fence, garden, shingled walls and small dormers were typical of the domestic cottage styling for wayside depots of the period. Radio traffic control and centralized agencies have, unfortunately, closed most small stations like this since 1945.

ABOVE: Port Alberni, terminus of the branch from Parksville, in the 1930s. Carloads of lumber line the wharf, while in the foreground a trim 4-6-0 pauses at the station.

Excitement mounts as the first passenger train, from Victoria, rounds the bend and chugs triumphantly into Cowichan Lake station, on the 18th of June, 1913.

26

ABOVE: E&N log train of the 1920s. Sturdy 2-8-0s hauled most of the line's freight, from the late 1890s to the early 1940s.

Via diesel rail car 6133 approaches the Esquimalt sand tower for its daily ration, before commencing the morning run to Courtenay.

An 8000 class Baldwin diesel-electric road switcher rumbles over Arbutus Canyon with a work extra, about 1950. Thirteen of these 1,000 horsepower units arrived in 1948-49 to make the E&N the first fully dieselized division on the CPR.

# CANADIAN NATIONAL

The CNR is Canada's largest railway, with 25,000 miles (40,000 km) of track and well over 2,000 locomotives. This federally owned system serves all ten provinces and reaches into the North at Hay River, on Great Slave Lake, and Churchill, on Hudson Bay. Its related activities include hotels, real estate, telecommunications and ships.

Canadian National Railways was formed in 1917, when the Canadian Northern, a short-lived transcontinental built piecemeal by railway contractors Mackenzie and Mann, was taken over by Ottawa and combined with Canadian Government Railways, a recent amalgam of the Intercolonial Railway through the Atlantic provinces and the National Transcontinental, the eastern division of the Grand Trunk Pacific.

The GTPR's parent, the venerable Grand Trunk System, that had operated in Ontario and Quebec since the 1850s, missed the opportunity of building the CPR by insisting upon an American link between southern Ontario and the prairies. By the time the Grand Trunk did enter the West with its offshoot company, the southern areas were firmly in the hands of Canadian Pacific, while the northern prairies were well served by Canadian Northern. The Grand Trunk Pacific could offer little more than a shorter Edmonton-Winnipeg route and a connection to the new but secondary port of Prince Rupert. The war of 1914 found both the GTPR and the Canadian Northern financially overextended, incapable of withstanding the intense economic buffeting that was to ensue. One by one the companies fell into government ownership, starting with the repossession of the GTP's eastern division in 1915 (which had been built Moncton to Winnipeg at federal expense) and ending with the takeover of the Grand Trunk itself, in 1920.

Although the Canadian Northern and GTPR lines west of Edmonton to the Yellowhead Pass were largely combined during the First World War, when steel shortages became acute, most of the old routes elsewhere remained intact. The two eastern connecting lines are relatively unchanged, as are the diverging western routes from the Yellowhead to Vancouver and Prince Rupert.

The western lines of CN Rail are today divided into two main regions: Prairie, from Armstrong, Ontario to Biggar, Saskatchewan, and Mountain, from Biggar to the Pacific. Since 1945, many prairie branches have been abandoned and trackage on Vancouver Island has shrunk to almost nothing, but these reductions have been somewhat offset by expansion in the North, to Lynn Lake, Manitoba (1955) and Great Slave Lake, N.W.T. (1965), lease of the Alberta Resources Railway (1969) and purchase of full ownership of the Northern Alberta Railways Company (1981).

Range and effectiveness of the CNR has been further increased through cooperation with other railways. The Okanagan Valley line, built in the mid 1920s set the tone, with CN granting running rights over its new Vernon-Kelowna rails to Canadian Pacific, in exchange for access to them via CP from Kamloops. In more recent years, blockage of mainlines by snow, derailments, etc., has been nicely overcome by mutual rerouting arrangements, CN trains moving through Rogers Pass, CP's going by way of the Yellowhead. Intercompany relations have become so cordial that CPR grain trains have even found their way to Churchill, CN's exclusive preserve, and freight sharing arrangements such as the joint CN–BCR service to the northeast coal fields of British Columbia are becoming commonplace.

The tremendous growth in resource industries has necessitated major improvements to western mainlines since the mid 1970s. In the preceeding decade, the average number of trains per day had risen from 10 to 26, weight per car increased from 40 tons to between 75 and 100 and the usual number of cars per freight had gone from 50 to 87. A vigorous double tracking program had to be undertaken, rail strength increased (to as much as 136 pound), ballast deepened, concrete crossties installed and siding lengths doubled, to about 7,000 feet each. The increase in locomotive horsepower in the period 1960-1980 was no less spectacular, going from 1,200 and 1,700 to 3,000 h.p. per unit.

The single, relatively low (3,712 foot) summit at the Yellowhead has saved the railway enormous amounts of money in fuel, equipment and tunnelling costs. All tunnels on the CNR are quite short and unless total double tracking is required there will be little need for more in the future. The 11,200 foot bore through Burnaby mountain in 1969 was one of the rare projects of this sort in recent years.

Coal, sulphur, potash, grain and forest products form the bulk of CNR freight in western Canada. Lumber has been the single best revenue earner lately and eleven thousand cars, the largest fleet in North America, is devoted to its movement. Pulp for newsprint is another major item, accounting for some 50,000 boxcar loads per annum in the 1980s. Grain, whose movement caused a three hundred million dollar loss to the company in 1982, began to be more profitable following abolition of the Crow Rate in 1984 but still compares poorly with other goods in terms of revenue.

Like the CPR, Canadian National gave up its passenger business to VIA RAIL in 1978. Before that, some effort had been made to attract patronage through the introduction of the vista-domed Supercontinental, on the Vancouver–Toronto/Montreal run. It was partially successful but trimming of feeder routes and schedules reduced rail's practicability generally. The Supercontinental was dropped by VIA in 1981, then revived in 1985 but it is unlikely that any passenger service will long survive without a complete modernization of the sort seen in Europe and Japan.

CN Rail will no doubt continue to modernize its own operations with or without VIA. Innovations that began with the world's first passenger train radios in 1923 have continued into the present, ranging from more comfortable wide-nosed locomotive cabs in the 1960s to remote-controlled switching engines in the '80s. The only remaining major updating would appear to be electrification, a step advocated in the Canadian Senate as far back as 1920.

CNR's crest of 1927 to 1960, which was based upon an earlier Grand Trunk design.

# CNR CHRONOLOGY for Western Lines

1880 — The Winnipeg & Hudson Bay Rwy. & Steamship Co. and the Nelson Valley Rwy. & Transportation Co. incorporate 7 May.

1883 — W&HBR&S and the NVR&T companies amalgamate to become the Winnipeg & Hudson Bay Railway Co. 25 May.

1889 — Manitoba Govt. leases its Red River Valley Rwy. (Winnipeg to Emerson) to Northern Pacific. Opened 1 September it becomes the Northern Pacific & Manitoba Rwy. Co.

1894 — W&HBR changes name to Winnipeg Great Northern Rwy. Co.

1899 — WGNR and the Lake Manitoba Rwy. & Canal Co. amalgamate as the Canadian Northern Rwy. Co.
— Canadian Northern acquires the Port Arthur, Duluth & Western Rwy.
— Minnesota & Manitoba R.R. (C.Nor. owned) incorporates 12 April.

1900 — Manitoba & South Eastern Rwy. (southeast from Winnipeg) amalgamated with Canadian Northern on 3 May.
— Ontario & Rainy River Rwy. amalgamated with C.Nor. 4 May.

1901 — Northern Pacific's NP&M, Portage & North Western, Winnipeg Transfer Co. and Waskada & North Eastern railways leased to the Manitoba Government for 999 years 15 January, then assigned to Canadian Northern on 23 May.

1903 — Morden & North Western Rwy. amalgamated with C.Nor. 21 Feb.
— Western Extension Rwy. amalgamated with Canadian Northern 23 October.
— Grand Trunk Pacific Rwy. incorporated on 24 October.

1905 — GTPR sod turning near Carberry, Manitoba 29 August.
— First Canadian Northern train into Edmonton 23 November.

1906 — Qu'Appelle, Long Lake & Saskatchewan Rwy. acquired by C.Nor. 14 December.

1908 — GTP construction eastward from Prince Rupert begun in autumn.
— Edmonton, Yukon & Pacific Rwy. amalgamated with Canadian Northern 7 May.

1909 — Alberta Midland, Saskatchewan North Western and the Northern Extension Rwy. amalgamated with Canadian Northern in June and August.

1910 — Canadian Northern construction begins eastward from New Westminster, B.C.
— Saskatchewan Midland Rwy. amalgamated with C.Nor. 9 May.
— Hudson Bay line built from Hudson Bay Jct. to The Pas.

1911 — Edmonton & Slave Lake Rwy. amalgamated with Canadian Northern 20 February.

1913 — Winnipeg & Northern Rwy. amalgamated with C.Nor. on 2 June.
— Last spike on the National Transcontinental (GTPR's East Div.) driven 17 November.

1914 — First Canadian Northern train into Calgary 23 February.
— First Grand Trunk Pacific train into Calgary 27 February.
— Last Spike on the GTPR driven near Ft. Fraser, B.C. on 7 April.
— First Grand Trunk Pacific train to Prince Rupert 8 April.

1915 — Last Spike on C.Nor. driven at Basque, B.C. (Thompson River Canyon) 23 January.
— Canadian Government Railways organized in June to operate the National Transcontinental jointly with the Intercolonial Rwy.

1917 — Canadian Northern and CGR combined and named Canadian National Railways on 20 December.

1919 — Federal government takes over the Grand Trunk Pacific, 10 March.

1920 — Federal government takes over the parent Grand Trunk System, 21 May.

1926 — First locomotive built in Western Canada, CNR No. 2747, leaves Transcona shops.

1927 — Hudson Bay line, The Pas to Churchill (510 miles) completed.

1929 — Northern Alberta Railways acquired, in partnership with the CPR.

1948 — First production model diesel-electric locomotives, 1500 h.p. EMD F3 units, arrive 27 May.

1955 — Lynn Lake extension completed (Sherridon branch built 1930).

1964 — First ore shipments from Pine Point, on Great Slave Lake, begin in November.

1969 — Thornton tunnel built through Burnaby mountain to Second Narrows bridge.
— Alberta Resources Railway leased. Opening ceremonies 28 May.

1975 — Last CN ship on the Pacific coast, the SS Prince George III burns.

1976 — CN becomes the first railway in Canada to use concrete ties.

1981 — Full ownership of Northern Alberta Railways, beginning 1 January.

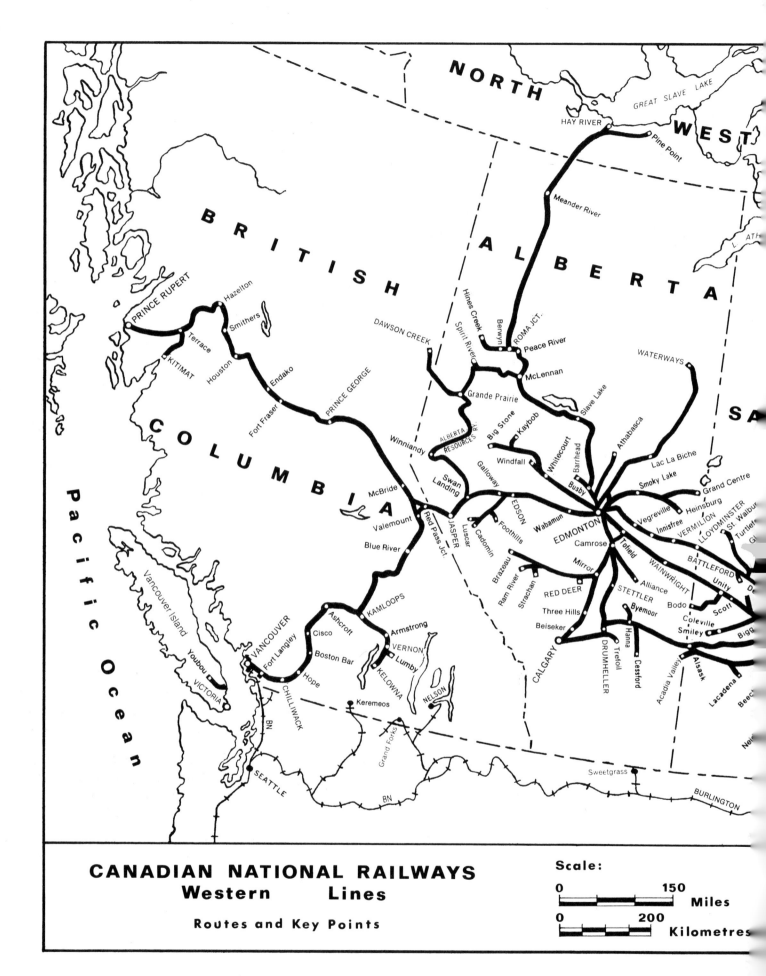

# CANADIAN NATIONAL RAILWAYS
## Western Lines
### Routes and Key Points

Scale:

0 ————————— 150 **Miles**

0 ————————— 200 **Kilometres**

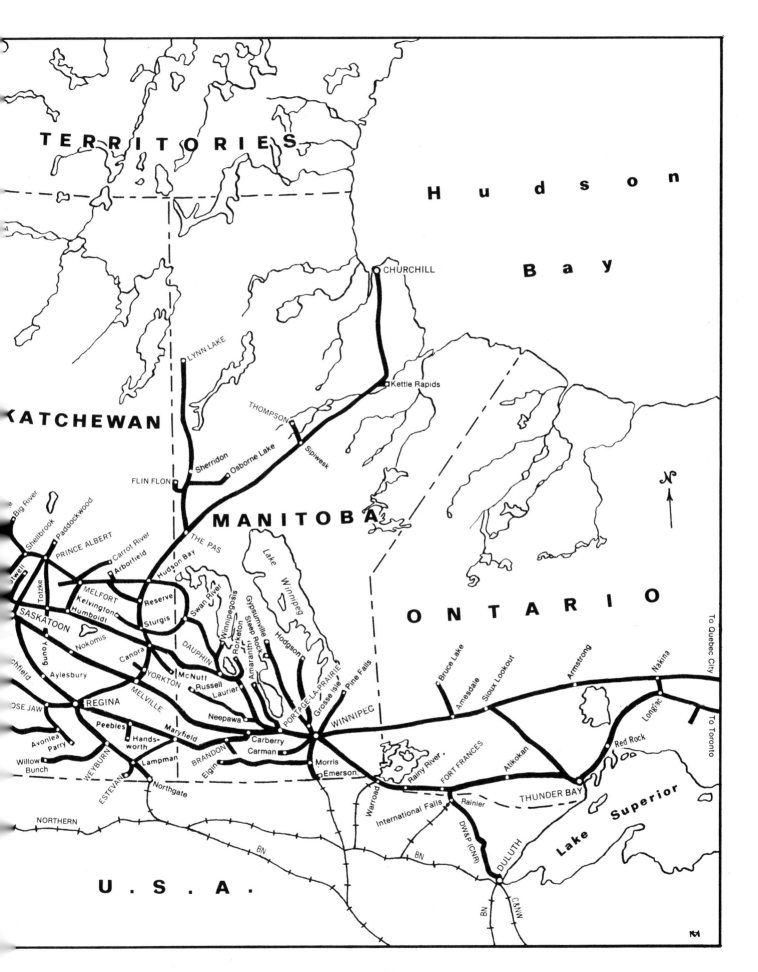

TOP RIGHT: Mountain type 4-8-2 number 6029, built in 1924 at Kingston, Ontario for the CNR. Many of its class served in the West and were converted from coal to oil-burning after World War II, ending much back-breaking labor for their firemen. With dieselization, firemen disappeared altogether from freight train crews.

LEFT: The first train into Edmonton, 20 October 1902. The Edmonton, Yukon & Pacific Railway only grew to be a nine mile link to Strathcona, across the river. In 1907, it was absorbed into the Canadian Northern but in 1954 its tracks were abandoned.

RIGHT: CNR 2141, originally a Canadian Northern engine, built in Kingston and the last CN steam locomotive to run on Vancouver Island (4 July 1958). It is seen here at Kamloops, where it was placed on display in 1961.

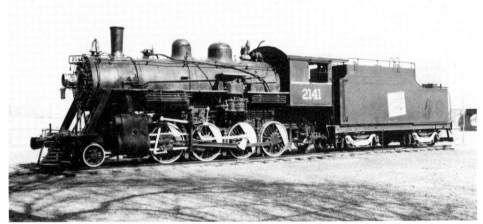

LOWER LEFT: Scene of circa 1920 at The Pas, Manitoba. To the left of number 420, an ex-McArthur Co. 2-6-0, lies a two-stall roundhouse, while to the right is the station and water tower. The Pas was the end of steel for the Hudson Bay line from 1910 to 1927.

RIGHT: Bullet-nosed 6060, an MLW product of 1944 built for fast passenger service on the Montreal-Toronto line. In 1955, when diesels took over there, 6060 was converted to oil burning and sent west. The CNR retired all its steam power on 31 December 1960 but 6060 was made a display piece at Jasper, Alberta until 1972, when it was recalled to special excursion duties in the East. In 1980, it once again returned West, to Edmonton and the care of the Alberta Pioneer Rail Association.

ABOVE: The imposing passenger terminal at Vancouver, B.C. A lack of funds in
1915 prevented the building of a long approach tunnel. Running rights over the Great
Northern's tracks were secured instead and have been used ever since.

BELOW: Reclining, well upholstered seats aboard an ex-CNR,VIA RAIL Daynighter
coach. Footrests and fold-out trays add extra comfort and convenience.

Contrasts in passenger service:

UPPER LEFT: Wooden plat-
forms, gas lamps and truss-rod
coaches at Grand Trunk
Pacific's Tofield, Alta., about
1914, when a branch ran south
from here to Calgary.

LOWER LEFT: CN's smooth,
steel Supercontinental at Blue
River, B.C. circa 1975. Behind it
rises the radio traffic control
tower, a far cry from the
mechanical oval order board
seen in the previous Tofield
picture.

ABOVE: Continuous welded rail, in 1,440-foot lengths, in transit from the Winnipeg yards. By reducing the number of rail joints (standard rail is only 39 feet, or 12 metres long) travel is made smoother and wear to wheels and rails significantly lessened. Was continuous welded rail the inspiration for CN's recent logo? Probably not, but the spaghetti-like similarity is striking.

BELOW: Grinding rail on the upper Fraser River mainline, to eliminate irregularities, corrosion and engine burns. Equipment includes several grinder cars, food, fuel and housing for the crew. With to-day's heavy traffic, grinding must be done up to four times a year.

ABOVE: An articulated 108-ton covered grain hopper car, built at the Transcona Shops in 1985 for trial on the boggy, unstable line to Churchill. By spreading weight over three trucks instead of two, greater loads are possible per track segment.

RIGHT: Saskatchewan potash being transferred to a lake freighter at Thunder Bay. Potash was discovered on the prairies in 1943, during oil exploration, and has since become a major freight item for the railways. About 90% is used for fertilizer. The rest goes into glass, china, soap, matches, dyes, TV tubes, rubber, photographic film, insecticides and pharmaceuticals.

ABOVE: Clover Bar Bridge, over the North Saskatchewan River east of Edmonton. Built by the Grand Trunk Pacific in 1908, this 1,655 foot long structure testifies to the solidity of GTP building practices.

LEFT: A unit train of Alberta coal bound for Roberts Bank roars onto the BCR's Port Subdivision near Cloverdale, B.C. Other CN unit trains move coal, sulphur and potash to North Vancouver terminals.

Switcher 7156 pulling freight cars from a Seaspan ferry at Victoria, B.C. in October, 1981. Very little of the once extensive trackage on Vancouver Island was left by this time. The Saanich peninsula line was abandoned in 1935, the Victoria-Deerholme section in the late 1970s, and application had been made to abandon all but a small amount of industrial trackage at Cowichan Bay and Victoria.

RIGHT: End of a CNR freight train and possibly the end of an era. This scene at Wabamun, Alberta in the late 1970s may soon become a thing of the past. The pattern for removal of cabooses was set in 1982, when a nationwide U.S. rail-labour agreement was signed. The CNR applied soon afterward for permission to test cabooseless trains. An electronic box with flasher light and airbrake pressure monitor mounted on the last freight car replaces the traditional "shack".

A large, wedge type snowplow of the Northern Alberta Railways awaits the call to duty at Edmonton. Although snowfall is not excessive in this region, strong winds can pile up concrete-hard drifts ten to twenty feet high and perhaps a half mile long.

## THE GREAT SLAVE LAKE RAILWAY

The GSLR was built by the Canadian Government in 1962–65 to connect Hay River, in the Northwest Territories, with Roma Junction, on the NAR in Alberta. Its aim was to develop area oil, gas and agriculture, tap the sizeable lead and zinc deposits at Pine Point, and provide a simpler route for Arctic freight destined for Mackenzie River boats, Hay River replacing Waterways, Alberta. Construction and operation of the 377 mile line was assigned to the Canadian National Railways and the GSLR became part of CN's Peace River division.

## THE ALBERTA RESOURCES RAILWAY

An Alberta Government project, the ARR was built through rugged mountain foothill wilderness between 1965 and 1969, then leased to the CNR. From a junction with the NAR at Grande Prairie, the line winds 233 miles south to the CNR mainline at Swan Landing, between Hinton and Jasper. The ARR has no equipment of its own. The CNR supplies everything necessary to move coal from Grande Cache, wood pulp from the Grande Prairie area, etc., to southern markets.

# NORTHERN ALBERTA RAILWAYS

For almost seventy years the Northern Alberta Railways Company and its predecessors brought southward the wealth of forest products, minerals, grain and livestock that lay to the north of Edmonton. Moreover, its 920 miles of mainline carried all manner of supplies necessary for the development and sustenance of the region all the way to the Arctic, an area almost devoid of roads. Interchanges occurred with the Great Slave Lake Railway near Peace River, the BCR at Dawson Creek, the Alberta Resources Railway at Grande Prairie, and both the CN and CPR at Edmonton. Passenger service was very basic, generally only by mixed freight/passenger train, but for many people it was the sole link with the outside world. It was not uncommon for NAR trains to stop for individuals, or to deliver to them their mail, groceries and medicines.

Like its present owner, Canadian National Railways, the NAR was largely composed of lines bankrupted by the war of 1914. All three of the major constituents, the Edmonton, Dunvegan & BC Railway (running from Edmonton northwest to Spirit River), the Alberta & Great Waterways (from just north of Edmonton to Lac La Biche) and the Central Canada Railway (from McLennan to Peace River) belonged to the J.D. McArthur Co., of Winnipeg but by 1920 it became necessary to cede ownership to the Alberta Government.

The Canadian Pacific began operating the ED&BC and the CCR in 1920 but six years later returned them to the Alberta Government, who had been operating the A&GW line. Various extensions were made over the years and a completely new Pembina Valley Railway, from Busby to Barrhead, was built in 1926. The entire lot was then sold jointly to the CPR and CNR in 1929, when it became the Northern Alberta Railways Company. After that, the CP and CNR alternated in the yearly appointment of an operating manager and supplied equipment and expertise as needed.

The early years were not easy for the fledgling NAR, for as almost everyone knows the economy moved at a crawl through the 1930s. Business boomed for the railway in 1942, however, when the Alaska Highway, north from Dawson Creek, was undertaken. The number of locomotives had to be increased from 16 to 41 in order to cope with the surge in both freight and passenger traffic. The Canol project followed shortly afterwards and activity remained fairly brisk until the late 1950s, when the Peace River area was invaded by the Pacific Great Eastern. New highway construction also hit NAR business at this time and little relief came until the completion of the Great Slave Lake Railway in the mid 1960s, which brought considerable ore traffic from Pine Point mines. Oil extraction plant construction at Fort MacMurray at the end of the decade and following further boosted NAR fortunes, though passenger service shrank to the Edmonton–Waterways line only.

The sale of Canadian Pacific's share in the NAR to the Canadian National Railways in 1980 spelled the end for the venerable company. NAR Edmonton facilities, many of them only a few years old, were vacated one by one. The dispatching office was transferred to CN's Calder Yards, engine sheds were demolished, station and offices closed. A new cut-off built between CN's Coronado Subdivision and the NAR line near Kerensky rerouted trains on the Lac La Biche run and black paint, appropriately enough, blotted out NAR insignia on locomotives as the company quietly vanished into the vast transcontinental system.

Dunvegan Yards, on the St. Albert Trail in Northwest Edmonton, seen from the roof of the diesel sheds in 1972. The station and freight sheds lie at centre left, in the background.

## NAR CHRONOLOGY

1907 — Edmonton, Dunvegan & B.C. Railway incorporated.
(Note: Dunvegan was never reached).
1909 — Alberta & Great Waterways Railway incorporated.
1912 — ED&BC construction begun.
1913 — Control of A&GWR acquired by J.D. McArthur Co.
— Central Canada Railway incorporated.
1916 — Rycroft–Grande Prairie branch completed.
— Carbondale–Lac La Biche line completed.
1920 — Alberta Govt. takes over all of the above.
— Canadian Pacific operates ED&BC and the CCR.
1924 — Wembley extension completed.
1925 — Waterways connected in November.
1926 — Alberta Govt. operates all the railways.
1927 — Pembina Valley Rwy. completed (Busby–Barrhead).
1928 — Hythe extension completed.
1929 — NAR incorporated June 14th.
1930 — Dawson Creek and Fairview–Hines Creek extensions complete.
1958 — Dieselization begun, completed 1960.
1962 — Great Slave Lake Rwy. begun, completed 1964–65.
1967 — Tar sands oil extraction plant built at Ft. MacMurray.
1973 — NAR Headquarters move to new Dunvegan Yards offices.
1981 — Canadian National Rwys. becomes sole owner January 1st.

RIGHT: Preserved NAR steam power in action on the Alberta Pioneer Railway Association's trackage in Edmonton. Locomotive 73, a 2-8-0 built in 1927 at Kingston, Ontario burns oil and like many Canadian locomotives made after 1911, has an all-weather, vestibule cab. Temperatures commonly drop to 40 degrees below zero on the prairies and engines can freeze to the rails so solidly that a bump from another locomotive may be required to free them. The NAR owned as many as 41 steam locos during the Second World War but in normal times about 16 sufficed. Size ranged from small switchers to heavy 2-10-0 freights. The last of them worked in 1960.

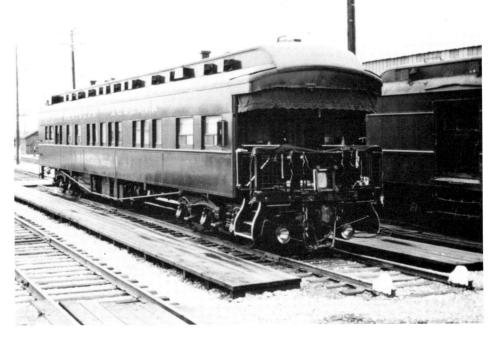

LOWER RIGHT: NAR business car **Peace River**, equipped with low-mounted lights for track inspection. Both the immaculately kept coach and the baggage car to the right of it are classics of the 1920s.

The Northern Alberta Railways diesel fleet, totalling 21 units in 1980, included several General Motors GMD 1 models. These 1200 hp road switchers, unique to the NAR and CNR, had unpowered middle axles in their trucks. The centre wheels were intended only to better distribute weight of the locomotive over the rail, much of which is laid over soggy muskeg.

Despite ownership by the two huge transcontinentals for over fifty years, the NAR managed to maintain its own distinct individuality. The bay window caboose at left is just one of many examples.

The unusual combination coach-caboose at left brought up the rear on many NAR mixed freight/passenger trains. Its Austrian styled bay window, similar to the one on the caboose above, improved the conductor's view of the cars ahead without requiring him to mount into a cupola. After Canadian National became sole owner of the NAR in 1981, these cars were replaced with a regular caboose and CN coach on the twice-weekly **Muskeg Mixed** to Waterways.

# BURLINGTON NORTHERN

In 1970, after close relations dating back to the turn of the century, when they jointly acquired the Chicago, Burlington & Quincy, the Great Northern and the Northern Pacific, along with their subsidiaries, the CB&Q and the Spokane, Portland & Seattle railways merged to form the Burlington Northern Railroad. Some subsequent acquisitions have extended lines southward to Mobile, Pensacola and Galveston, on the Gulf of Mexico, and a 1985 agreement with Canadian National Railways makes possible virtual single line service over both these giant systems.

Burlington Northern's own Canadian operations are today very limited but connections to Vancouver, Huntingdon, Nelson, Sweet Grass, Northgate, Winnipeg and International Falls (see CP and CN maps) greatly facilitate Canada–United States freight movement. Forest products and fertilizer (potash and sulphur) top the list of southbound items, while northbound freight involves mainly manufactured goods and coke, the latter from oil refineries at Cherry Point, on the Washington coast. Passenger service was taken over by Amtrak, the American government's agency, in 1970 and the last of it, between Vancouver and Seattle, was discontinued in September 1981.

The BN's predecessor companies, GN and NPR were once prominent in the Canadian West. Northern Pacific built a small network of lines in southern Manitoba, beginning in 1888. Westward expansion included construction of the Midland Railway in 1903, in partnership with the Great Northern but financial reverses eventually led to most NPR Canadian holdings being passed to either Great Northern or the Canadian Northern (now Canadian National Railways).

The Great Northern, under the aggressive leadership of James J. Hill, an ex-patriate Canadian, endeavoured to divert Canadian raw materials to industries south of the border. In addition to the Midland operations alluded to above, which linked Winnipeg, Portage la Prairie, Morden and several other small farm communities, GN began a Brandon, Saskatchewan & Hudson Bay railway. By 1906, rails were laid from St. John, North Dakota to Brandon but little else of the great scheme was ever accomplished. Manitoba lines were abandoned in stages until by 1937 only the Winnipeg yards remained, with trackage rights to them over the CNR from the border.

In British Columbia, Hill's attention focussed on minerals in the southeastern part of the province. The Kaslo & Slocan, a narrow gauge line, was sponsored in the early 1890s to tap lead and silver deposits, while in 1901 Kootenay coal prompted the building of the Crow's Nest Southern from Rexford, Montana to Fernie, Michel and Elko, B.C. The K & S passed eventually to GN's arch rival, the Canadian Pacific, and the CNS like most of the Great Northern's other lines in the province, was abandoned. What has survived includes the Nelson & Fort Sheppard Railway, built in 1893 and taken over by GN five years later, part of the Washington & Great Northern Railway, begun in 1901 and which briefly cuts into Canada near Keremeos, and the remnants of the Vancouver, Westminster and Yukon, the New Westminster Southern and the Victoria Terminal & Ferry Company, built between 1891 and 1909, that lead from downtown Vancouver through White Rock to Blaine, Washington.

Two of the few Burlington Northern locomotives working in Canada, numbers 390 and 391, at New Westminster, B.C. The nose to nose operation and roof-mounted revolving flashers are peculiarities on this side of the border.

## BNR CHRONOLOGY relevant to present Canadian operations

1862 — St. Paul & Pacific R.R. begins operation, 2 July.
1870 — Northern Pacific Railway construction begun.
1879 — St. P&P becomes the St. Paul, Minneapolis & Manitoba Rwy.
1881 — James J. Hill buys the Minneapolis & St. Cloud R.R.
1883 — NPR completed lakehead to Portland. Last spike at Gold Creek, Montana, 8 Sept.
1889 — The M&ST.C. becomes the Great Northern Railway.
1890 — The St.P., M&M Rwy. is merged into the Great Northern.
1891 — GN's New Westminster Southern, from Liverpool (opposite New Westminster, on the south bank of the Fraser) to Blaine via Cloverdale, opens 14 Feb.
1893 — Nelson & Fort Sheppard Railway (Nelson — Waneta) built.
     — Last spike on the Great Northern line to the Pacific driven 6 January, at Scenic, Washington.
1898 — Nelson & Fort Sheppard Rwy. becomes Great Northern property.
1901 — Washington & Great Northern Rwy. built through the Kettle Valley to Canada (Keremeos).
1903 — Midland Railway begun in Manitoba jointly by NP and GNR.
     — Vancouver, Westminster & Yukon Rwy. (New Westminster-Vancouver) built.
1909 — New shoreline route of the Victoria Terminal & Ferry Co., from Blaine through White Rock, replaces the Blaine–Cloverdale line.
     — Great Northern becomes sole owner of the Midland Rwy. Co.
1970 — NP, GN, CB&Q and SP&S merge to form Burlington Northern, 2 March.
     — Amtrak takes over passenger services.
1981 — Last Amtrak train, Vancouver-Seattle, 30 September.

ABOVE: A westbound grain train behind three bright red CP Rail diesel-electrics ducks under the Trans-Canada Highway near Golden, B.C., on its long journey to the sea.

RIGHT: Canadian Pacific's **Carrier Princess** glides into Vancouver harbour loaded with freight cars, containers and highway trailers from Nanaimo. This ferry constitutes the main link between the Esquimalt & Nanaimo Railway and the mainland.

ABOVE: A Canadian National ballast train engaged in the massive track improvement program between Edmonton and Vancouver. BELOW: Northern Alberta Railways station at McLennan. Straw yellow roofs and bluejean colored walls give a decidedly prairie allure.

ABOVE: The BC Hydro Railway's main yards in New Westminster/Burnaby, built on reclaimed peat bog at the foot of Trapp Road in 1965.

RIGHT: British Columbia Railway's 6,000 hp GF60 electric locomotive, one of seven built in 1984 for the Tumbler Ridge branchline by General Motors, in London, Ontario. Technology and electrical parts were supplied by ASEA, of Sweden. The 82 mile (129 km) line has four tunnels, one of them 5.6 miles (9 km) long. By using 50,000 volt alternating current, only a single substation was required. Millions of dollars were also saved on tunnel ventilation through the choice of electric over diesel operation.

ABOVE: Number 73 trailing a long white plume as it streaks toward White Pass with WP&Y's last excursion, on 30 August 1982.

BELOW: White Pass & Yukon mixed consist by Fraser Lake, southbound to Skagway, Alaska. Its MLW-built locomotives date to 1969-71.

ABOVE: Greater Winnipeg Water District Railway excursion at Indian Bay, in 1981. Engine No. 100 began the line's dieselization in 1946.

BELOW: Pacific Elevators' small, British-built Hunslet diesels B and C, at the Vancouver terminal. Note the distinctly European side rods and large wheels.

ABOVE: A Canfor log train on the Noomis Creek trestle, bound for Beaver Cove, Vancouver Island.

BELOW: Comox Logging & Railway Company's No. 11, the 1923 Baldwin that ended steam logging on the Nanaimo Lakes line.

ABOVE: Electric transportation's cleanliness admirably demonstrated at Edmonton's Clareview station.

BELOW: Calgary's 7th Avenue mall, where traffic is restricted to transit vehicles. Coaches and overhead catenary for both Calgary and Edmonton systems were of West German design.

VRRT's Nanaimo St. station, by A. Parker Associates/Architektengruppe U-Bahn. Modular hoop construction and transparency are characteristic of the line's surface stations. Drawing by Ron Love.

Cheerful interior of a Vancouver ALRT coach. Seating capacity is 40, standee space 35. The red, white and blue color scheme is now standard for all BC-owned railway equipment.

# THE BRITISH COLUMBIA RAILWAY

With approximately fourteen hundred miles of mainline, the BCR ranks as the third largest railway in Canada. It stands number one amongst regionals and is contained entirely within the province of British Columbia, by whom it is owned.

Although the BCR has enjoyed a measure of prosperity in recent years, such has not always been the case. Begun as a privately owned resource development line in 1912, under the name Pacific Great Eastern, it soon encountered financial difficulty. With rail connecting only a coastal village to a sparsely-settled mountainous interior, and badly needed capital dried up by the war in Europe, ownership had to be passed from its builders, Foley, Welch & Stewart, to the Provincial Government in 1918.

Construction continued after that to a few miles beyond Quesnel, reached in 1921, but another thirty-one years passed before the PGE's original objective, Prince George was attained. Economic depression and a second world war in the interim brought hardships so severe that passengers sometimes had to use umbrellas when travelling in PGE coaches. Offers to purchase the line, which included one by the United States in 1945 (with an Alaska connection in mind) all came to nothing.

The 1952 completion of track to Prince George revived the struggling company. The new interchange with the Canadian National Railways not only brought more business but allowed rerouting of trains in emergencies involving blocked lines.

The 1956 filling of the gap in the PGE between North Vancouver and Squamish further improved the railway's viability. Freight barges had until then taken up to 24 hours for the 40 mile trip, and damage to cars was not rare in the course of car transfer, particularly at the Squamish dock.

Operating profits began to appear in the late 1950s and the PGE confidently expanded northward, reaching Fort St. John and Dawson Creek in 1958, Mackenzie and Fort St. James in the 1960s, Fort Nelson in 1971. Lumber, pulp, paper and other forest products now flowed in vast quantities as the world economy boomed. At this point, in 1972, the company's name was changed to British Columbia Railway and a bold new extension begun northwest towards Dease Lake. Unfortunately, market demand for the minerals intended to be exploited in that region fell substantially soon afterward and work on the line was suspended in 1977 at Chipmunk, 175 miles short of the objective.

Two new subdivisions were added after that, each very distinctive. One was the Port Sub, running from a BC Hydro Railway connection near Cloverdale, to the bulk freight terminal at Roberts Bank. It is separated from the rest of the BCR by several miles and no BCR trains run on it. All traffic on this, the former BC Harbours Board Railway, is comprised of coal and coke trains of the Canadian Pacific, Canadian National, and the Burlington Northern railways, but movement is controlled by the BCR dispatcher in North Vancouver.

The other important addition was the Tumbler Ridge branch line, built to carry coal from new mines in the northeast. It became the first long-distance heavy (50,000 volts) electric railway in the country. Long unit trains began to roll over its continuous welded rail to Prince George at the end of 1983. The CNR takes over for the remainder of the journey to the sea at Prince Rupert.

Traffic control for the whole of the BCR is by microwave radio. Long-distance use of this interference-free system was pioneered by the railway. In addition, a unique Locate, Identify and Control system, which eliminates the need for lineside signals while doing what its name implies, has been developed in an endless search for better efficiency.

Passenger operations, handled by diesel rail cars in recent years, have never extended beyond the North Vancouver to Prince George portion of the railway. In winter, skiers fill trains bound for Whistler, while in summer a steam-powered excursion along Howe Sound to Squamish is popular. Magnificent scenery has long been an attraction for the railway year round.

Being a mountain railroad, the BCR faces perennial problems with nature. Jiggers (four-wheel scooters) must precede trains in some sections, for rock often falls onto the tracks. Heavy snowfalls require constant winter plowing to prevent closures like that of 1916, which lasted three months. Moose taking advantage of the conveniently cleared train tracks present yet more headaches and in spring there is an epidemic of washouts. In the end the railway wins its battles with the insistent adversary, however, for perseverance has become a hallmark of this, the most dauntless of Canadian lines.

## BCR CHRONOLOGY

1912 — Incorporation as the Pacific Great Eastern Railway Feb. 27th.
      — Acquisition of the 9 mile Howe Sound & Northern Rwy.
1915 — Lines completed Squamish to Lillooet, N. Vancouver to Whytecliffe.
1918 — Ownership passed to the Province of British Columbia.
1921 — Lillooet to Quesnel section opened.
1928 — North Vancouver to Whytecliffe service discontinued.
1948 — Dieselization begun.
1949 — Work on line north of Quesnel recommenced.
1952 — Line opened to Prince George in November.
1956 — North Vancouver to Squamish line opened August 2nd.
1957 — Dieselization completed.
1958 — Prince George to Chetwynd, Fort St. John and Dawson Creek opened to traffic in October.
1966 — Kennedy to Mackenzie spur opened in August.
1968 — Odell to Fort St. James branch opened August 1st.
1970 — Management and maintenance of the BC Harbours Board Rwy. begun.
1971 — Fort St. John to Fort Nelson line opened September 10th.
1972 — Name changed to British Columbia Railway April 1st.
      — West Vancouver cut-off tunnel built.
      — Dease Lake extension begun.
1974 — Royal Hudson excursions to Squamish begun.
1977 — Dease Lake extension work halted.
1981 — Tumbler Ridge branch begun.
1983 — Tumbler Ridge branch opened November 1st.
      — BC Harbours Board Railway assets acquired.
1984 — BCR's historic debt retired by the Province of B.C.

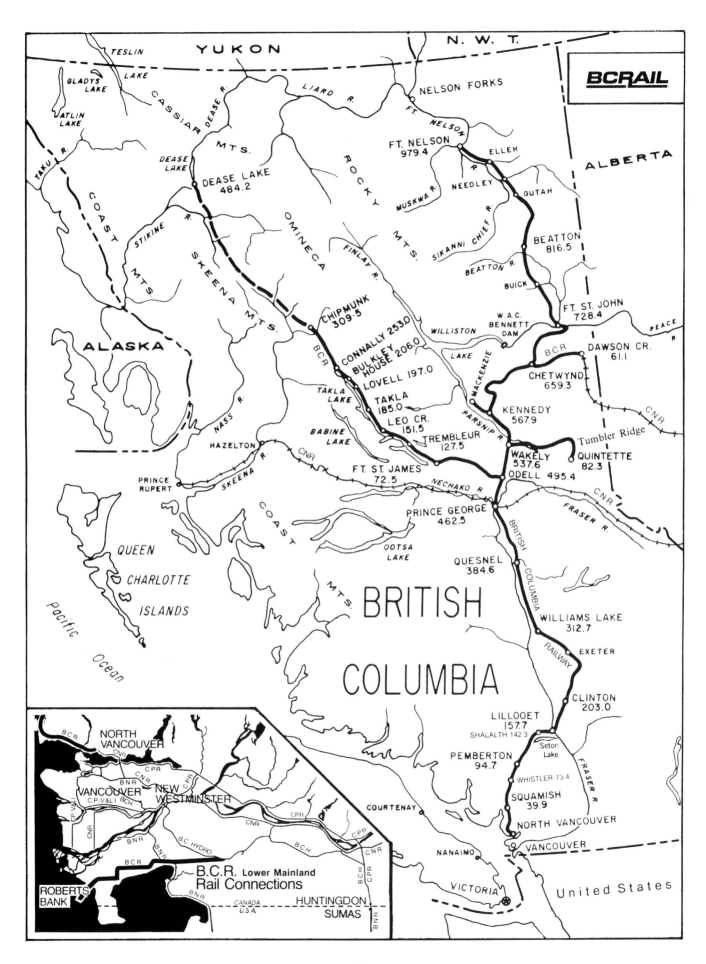

YUKON

N. W. T.

TESLIN LAKE

GLADYS LAKE

ATLIN LAKE

CASSIAR MTS.

DEASE R.

LIARD R.

NELSON FORKS

FT. NELSON

FT. NELSON 979.4

ELLEH

ALBERTA

TAKU R.

DEASE LAKE

DEASE LAKE 484.2

ROCKY MTS.

MUSKWA R.

NEEDLEY

GUTAH

SIKANNI CHIEF R.

BEATTON 816.5

BEATTON R.

BUICK

COAST MTS.

STIKINE R.

SKEENA MTS.

OMINECA

FINLAY R.

W.A.C. BENNETT DAM

FT. ST. JOHN 728.4

PEACE R.

ALASKA

CHIPMUNK 309.5

BCR

WILLISTON LAKE

BCR

DAWSON CR. 61.1

CONNALLY 253.0

BULKLEY HOUSE 206.0

LOVELL 197.0

MACKENZIE

CHETWYND 659.3

CNR

NASS R.

TAKLA LAKE

TAKLA 185.0

PARSNIP R.

KENNEDY 567.9

Tumbler Ridge

BABINE LAKE

LEO CR. 151.5

TREMBLEUR 127.5

WAKELY 537.6

QUINTETTE 82.3

HAZELTON

SKEENA R.

CNR

FT. ST. JAMES 72.5

NECHAKO R.

ODELL 495.4

CNR

PRINCE RUPERT

PRINCE GEORGE 462.5

FRASER R.

QUEEN CHARLOTTE ISLANDS

OOTSA LAKE

QUESNEL 384.6

BRITISH COLUMBIA

Pacific Ocean

MTS.

BRITISH COLUMBIA

WILLIAMS LAKE 312.7

RAILWAY

EXETER

CLINTON 203.0

LILLOOET 157.7

SHALALTH 142.3

Seton Lake

FRASER R.

PEMBERTON 94.7

COURTENAY

WHISTLER 73.4

SQUAMISH 39.9

NORTH VANCOUVER

NANAIMO

VANCOUVER

VICTORIA

United States

NORTH VANCOUVER

BCR

CNR

CPR

VANCOUVER

CP/V&LI

BCH

NEW WESTMINSTER

CPR

CNR

CPR

CNR

CP V&LI

BNR

BNR

BC HYDRO

BCR

BCH

CNR

CPR

BCH

CPR

CNR

B.C.R. Lower Mainland Rail Connections

ROBERTS BANK

BNR

CANADA U.S.A.

HUNTINGDON

SUMAS

Pacific Great Eastern's No. 1, built in 1874 by Manning Wardle, of Leeds, England. The little saddletanker hauled coal at Nanaimo and shifted lumber at Ladysmith before going to work for the Howe Sound & Northern Railway at Squamish, in 1908. It helped in PGE construction before being retired in 1919.

PGE caribou emblem of 1945 - 1965.

Prairie type steam locomotive No. 4, shunting at Squamish. It had the annoying habit of derailing and rolling onto its side, an act it put on in 1921, shortly before an official line inspection was due. Workers hurriedly covered her with brush and straw to avoid embarrassment. Number 4 and its twin, number 5, remained on the roster nevertheless until 1952, doing the lighter tasks.

Gasoline-powered car 107 with open observation coach 14 (a cut down ex-interurban) beside Seton Lake, in the early 1950s. The baggage compartment might contain anything from groceries to gold coming from local mines. Automobiles were often towed behind on flatcars, from Shalalth to Seton, in the days before a road was built in the area.

ABOVE: Passenger train on the Squamish dock, where steamship connection was made prior to completion of the rail link to North Vancouver in 1956. On the point is 2-8-0 number 53, which plunged into Seton Lake on a January night in 1950, taking with it both its engineer and fireman. It has never been located since.

BELOW: The morning train to Prince George awaits departure from North Vancouver. Two of its four coaches will be cut off at Lillooet and return the same evening. These refurbished Budd Diesel Rail Cars of the 1950s continued to provide comfortable travel through truly splendid scenery for decades.

LEFT: Number 551, the 65-ton General Electric switcher that began PGE dieselization in 1948. Its bright orange body contrasted sharply with the sober black of the steamers it replaced.

BELOW: BCR diesel 808 being recovered from the icy waters of Seton Lake, in May 1981, over a year after it hit a rockslide, derailed and went swimming. Its 190-ton running mate, No. 711, proved unretrievable and still rests 160 feet below the lake's surface.

RIGHT: The more orthodox method for washing locomotives, demonstrated at the North Vancouver engine sheds. The wide-nosed cab of No. 729, which houses kitchen and toilet facilities at the front, was a joint development of the CNR and the Montreal Locomotive Works.

RIGHT: BCR's first slug, S401 with master unit 601. The railway makes slug auxilliaries from worn standard locomotives, discarding the cab and diesel generator. A master unit nourishes and controls the slug's electric traction motors, which about double the total horsepower of the two-piece switcher.

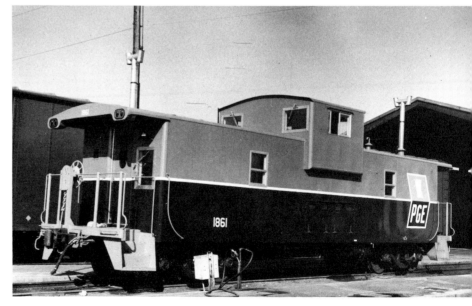

BOTTOM RIGHT: Modern steel caboose 1861, sporting the arrowhead herald used 1965-72. The broad, overhanging cupola affords optimum viewing to crews as they watch for signals, overheated bearings and dragging equipment. Built-in electric tail lights replace the kerosene marker lamps of old.

ABOVE: Lumber, wrapped in plastic, goes to market aboard a BCR bulkhead flat car. Forest products account for two-thirds of the railway's revenues and over 60 plants are served.

BELOW: Wood chips are emptied from high gondola cars at Fibreco, in North Vancouver. The cars are shunted in and out of the rotary dumper by the coupler-equipped, rubber-tired vehicle on the left.

RIGHT: Northeast B.C. coal at the Ridley Island terminal near Prince Rupert. Trains are moved through the rotary dumper by a mechanical indexer and emptied two at a time. There is no need to uncouple them to do so, for they are equipped with special rotateable couplers. The 100-ton cars were built in CN's Transcona shops, Winnipeg. Ownership is shared 75% by CNR, 25% by BCR. BC Rail handles the cars between Tumbler Ridge and Prince George, CN from there to the sea.

CENTRE RIGHT: Detail of rotateable coupler.

BELOW: Roberts Bank terminal, on BCR's Port Subdivision, south of Vancouver. Tandem rotary dumpers here unload a hundred-car unit train of coal in less than two hours. Only CPR, CNR and BNR trains use this facility, which is entirely cut off from the rest of the BCR.

BCR's dogwood emblem of 1972-86, based upon the official provincial flower.

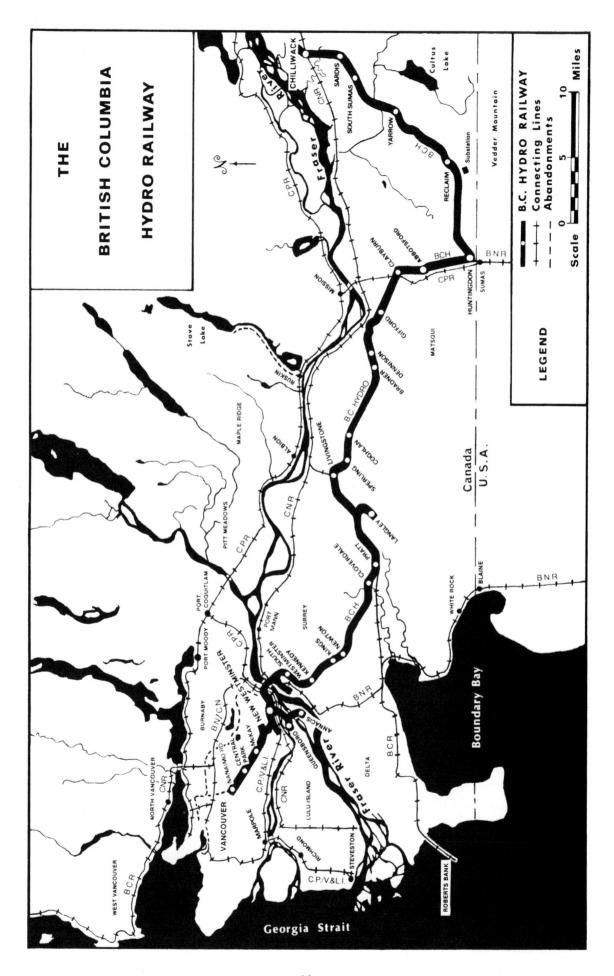

THE

BRITISH COLUMBIA

HYDRO RAILWAY

LEGEND

B.C. HYDRO RAILWAY
Connecting Lines
Abandonments

Scale

0          5          10
Miles

Georgia Strait

Boundary Bay

Canada
U.S.A.

Fraser River

Stave Lake

Cultus Lake

CHILLIWACK
SARDIS
SOUTH SUMAS
YARROW
RECLAIM
Substation
Vedder Mountain
ABBOTSFORD
CLAYBURN
MISSION
HUNTINGDON
SUMAS
BNR
GIFFORD
DENNISON
BRADNER
COGHLAN
LIVINGSTONE
SPERLING
RUSKIN
ALBION
MAPLE RIDGE
PITT MEADOWS
PORT COQUITLAM
PORT MOODY
LANGLEY
CLOVERDALE
PRATT
SURREY
NEWTON
KINGS
KENNEDY
PORT MANN
SOUTH WESTMINSTER
NEW WESTMINSTER
BURNABY
NANAIMO RD.
CENTRAL PARK
MCKAY
ANNACIS
QUEENSBORO
DELTA
LULU ISLAND
RICHMOND
STEVESTON
MARPOLE
VANCOUVER
NORTH VANCOUVER
WEST VANCOUVER
WHITE ROCK
BLAINE
ROBERTS BANK

CPR
CNR
BCH
BNR
BCR
C.P./V.&L.I.
B.C. HYDRO
BN/CN

66

# THE BC HYDRO RAILWAY

The British Columbia Hydro Railway's origins lie in electric railway and lighting companies formed in Vancouver a decade before the turn of the century. These and a bankrupt tramway connecting New Westminster to Vancouver were molded into the highly successful BC Electric Railway Company in 1897, by an able English financier named R.M. Horne-Payne. The BC Electric was so English that its Head Office was situated in London, England and dividends were paid in Pound Sterling. The company grew to become the largest interurban operator in Canada, and it ran streetcar lines as well in Vancouver, North Vancouver, New Westminster and Victoria. Nevertheless, by 1961 this sort of overt colonialism had become anachronistic and the company was liquidated to be replaced by a Province of B.C. crown corporation, known as BC Hydro.

Although the production of electricity, not petroleum, had always been an essential part of company operations, the BC Electric converted its railway from electric to diesel locomotion in 1958. This retrogressive act, which substituted noisy, polluting vehicles for clean, quiet ones must surely have caused some anguish to the railway's later owners, when oil prices skyrocketed in the 1970s.

Amongst the most significant changes that have taken place on the railway over the years was the discontinuance of passenger service in the 1950s. The whole character of the line quickly altered as stations and shelters were demolished and the human content of operations was reduced to a small staff dealing exclusively with carload freight. The closing of the Victoria-Deep Bay line in 1924 had relatively little impact on the overall operations and perhaps neither the dieselization mentioned above, nor the non-renewal of the Vancouver-Lulu Island Railway lease in 1985 can be seen to have so deeply affected the company's nature.

While the BCH is situated completely within the broad lower Fraser valley, there are several stiff grades, some as steep as 2.7 per cent along the line. It is a rambling route that traverses peaceful meadows as it wends its way from the Vancouver area southeastward to the U.S. border at Huntingdon, then back to the small city of Chilliwack, about a hundred miles in all.

In early years, the BC Electric hauled a considerable number of logs as the Fraser Valley was deforested and turned into farmland. Forest products continued to form over half of the BCER's traffic well into the 1950s but to-day that figure has dropped to only about a quarter, being largely composed of transfer cars of lumber, plywood, etc. from the BCR (via the CNR). Other freight handled by the line includes such things as ore concentrate and scrap metal, fertilizer, corn syrup (by the tank carload for lineside canneries), various manufactured goods and new automobiles and trucks moving to and from the huge port terminal on Annacis Island.

New Westminster is the main interchange point, for it is there that cars are exchanged with all three of the major railways, Canadian Pacific, Canadian National, and Burlington Northern. Additional connections are made with the CPR at Abbotsford, with CP and BN at Huntingdon, and with the CNR at Chilliwack. The variety and number of these locations has long made the BCHR exceptionally valuable for the transfer of Canada-United States freight in the Pacific region.

## BCE/BCHR CHRONOLOGY

1889 — Vancouver Electric Lighting Co. formed.
1890 — Vancouver Electric Railway & Light Co. formed.
1891 — Westminster & Vancouver Tramway Co. opens Central Park line.
1894 — Consolidated Railway & Light Co. formed from the VEL and the VER&L companies.
— Westminster & Vancouver Tramway Co. collapses.
1897 — BC Electric Railway Co. formed under R.M. Horne–Payne. Assets of Consolidated R&L and the W&V Tramway acquired.
1902 — Vancouver & Lulu Island Rwy. built by CPR Vancouver–Steveston.
1905 — V&LI Rwy. leased to the BCER and electrified.
1906 — Vancouver, Fraser Valley & Southern Rwy. incorporated.
1907 — VFV&SR acquired by BCER and construction begun.
1909 — Marpole to New Westminster line built by CPR and leased to BCER.
1910 — First regular passenger train to Chilliwack October 3rd.
1911 — Burnaby Lake Line opened June 12th.
1913 — Saanich Line (Victoria–Deep Bay) opened June 18th.
1923 — Stave Falls Rwy. (Stave Falls–Ruskin, on the CPR) acquired and electrified. It had been built by another power company in 1911 to serve the Stave Falls plant.
1924 — Saanich Line abandoned.
1944 — Stave Falls line abandoned.
1949 — Dieselization begun.
1950 — Passenger service to Chilliwack ends September 30th.
1952 — Vancouver Marpole passenger rail service dropped.
1953 — Burnaby Lake Line abandoned October 23rd.
1954 — Central Park Line passenger service ends.
1956 — Marpole–New Westminster passenger service ends.
1958 — Marpole–Steveston passenger service dropped. Dieselization complete.
1960 — Voluntary liquidation of BCER December 12th.
1961 — Formation of BC Hydro.
1965 — Trapp Yards completed.
1984 — BCHR headquarters moved from New Westminster to Langley.
1986 — V&LI lines returned to CPR after lease expires.

OPPOSITE LEFT: First downtown Vancouver BCER terminal, at Carrall and Hastings streets, ca. 1908. It was replaced by a much larger structure at the same location in 1911.

ABOVE: BCER steam engine No. 525, during track laying to Chilliwack in 1907-1910. Because of a power failure on opening day, the steamer also had the honor of hauling the first interurban train into the city. Steam locomotives were used on other segments of the BCER as well, before electrification.

BOTTOM RIGHT: Station at Tod Inlet, on the Saanich Peninsula line, Vancouver Island. It was a standard shelter design that saw use elsewhere, at Deep Bay (end of the line) for instance, and at stops on mainland routes (Glover, Sullivan, etc.), but the others did not have refreshment shacks like Tod Inlet's.

ABOVE: The Fraser River Bridge at New Westminster, built in 1902 by the province of B.C. and shared by the BCH, CN and BNR. The roadway seen in this early view was removed in 1937, when the Patullo Bridge was built alongside.

BELOW: A 1916 Fraser Valley milk train. Produce, fish, parcels, mail and newspapers also travelled in these light freight motors.

In 1908, the BC Electric built car shops on 12th Street, in New Westminster. Equipment was painted and repaired there until 1954 but for a few years at the beginning, trams and light locomotives were also manufactured. The last and perhaps finest of the BCER-built interurbans were these three arch and oval-windowed Connaught series cars, photographed when new in 1914.

RIGHT: The transformer substation at the foot of Vedder Mountain. The low, 600 volt direct current used by the BCER necessitated several substations along the line, all of them disguised as classical country villas. This and an identical one at Coughlin, between Langley and Abbotsford, were still standing in the 1980s, though no longer used for their original purposes.

ABOVE: The BCER's first freight motor, whose octagon-shaped cab was most unusual. Permanent headlights were not compulsory in 1910, when this photograph was taken, a sharp contrast with to-day's practice of running with them lit even in broad daylight.

## EARLY BC ELECTRIC FREIGHT EQUIPMENT

BELOW LEFT: The railway's very first caboose, a four-wheel bobber made in Seattle. The company used several of these, which were ideal for short runs where no bunks were needed for overnight crew accommodation.

BELOW RIGHT: Truss-rod boxcar 6148, a standard 40-foot wooden model of 1912. The expression "riding the rods" derived from the very dangerous practice of transients hitching a free ride by lying atop the truss rods.

ABOVE: BCER-built No. 951, little more than a motorized flatcar, with No. 973, one of five Baldwin-Westinghouse locos bought in 1913.

BELOW: No. 992, one of three British Dick Kerr models of 1909. Massive lateral hinges between the trucks prevented vertical movement, reducing cab stress and keeping all wheels down on the track.

ABOVE: Switcher 901 sorts cars by Trapp Yard Offices. Auto racks wait on the CNR interchange in the foreground.

LEFT: Unloading automobiles from eastern Canada at Annacis Island rail/sea terminal compound, where BCHR handles trainloads daily

UPPER RIGHT: Modern BCH diesel-electric freight locomotives at Huntingdon, where interchange is made with CP Rail and Burlington Northern.

LOWER RIGHT: Company-built caboose A-5, about to depart from New Westminster in 1986. Battery-powered tail lamps and heavy wire vandal-proof window screens are modern touches. The crew here is all male but females have also become conductors on the BCHR.

**MODERN BC HYDRO RAILWAY EQUIPMENT**

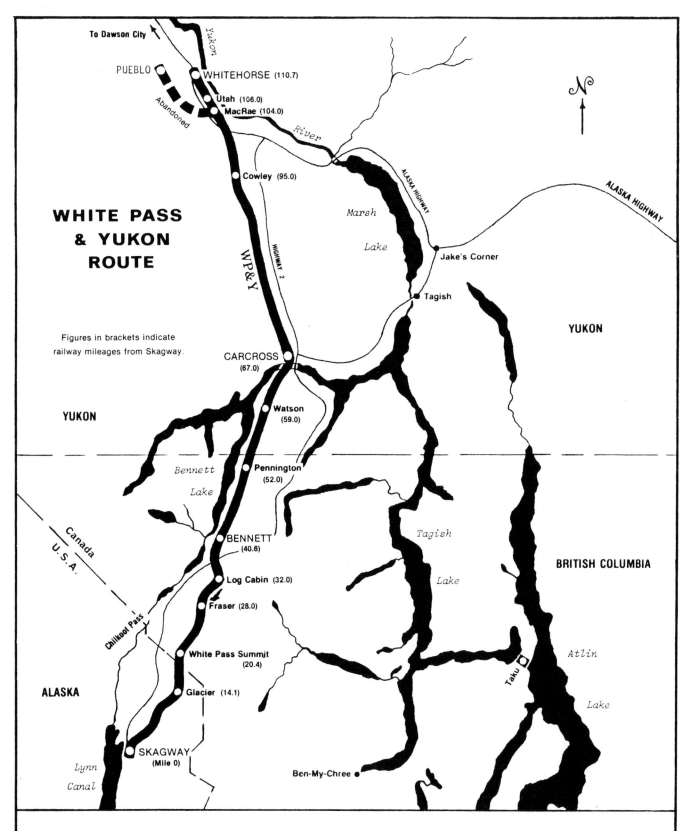

## WHITE PASS & YUKON ROUTE

Figures in brackets indicate railway mileages from Skagway.

To Dawson City

PUEBLO

WHITEHORSE (110.7)

Utah (106.0)

MacRae (104.0)

Abandoned

Yukon River

Cowley (95.0)

WP&Y

HIGHWAY 2

Marsh Lake

ALASKA HIGHWAY

ALASKA HIGHWAY

Jake's Corner

Tagish

YUKON

N

CARCROSS (67.0)

YUKON

Watson (59.0)

Bennett Lake

Pennington (52.0)

Tagish Lake

Canada

U.S.A.

BENNETT (40.6)

BRITISH COLUMBIA

Log Cabin (32.0)

Chilkoot Pass

Fraser (28.0)

White Pass Summit (20.4)

Taku

Atlin Lake

Glacier (14.1)

ALASKA

SKAGWAY (Mile 0)

Lynn Canal

Ben-My-Chree

The White Pass & Yukon required not less than three charters: one for the 20 miles over Alaskan territory, one for the 32 miles through British Columbia, and another for the remaining 58 miles to Whitehorse, where connection could be made via riverboat with Dawson, centre of the Klondike rush.

# THE WHITE PASS & YUKON ROUTE

When the 1896 discovery of Yukon gold brought thousands of people to the port of Skagway, Alaska, it became painfully evident that convenient transportation was needed over the massive rock barrier a scant few miles inland. Thus it was that Micheal J. Henry, a bold Irish-Canadian railway contractor and Thomas Tancrede, an adventurous British financier, agreed one night in a noisy Skagway saloon to build a narrow gauge railway over the redoubtable White Pass.

Begun at Skagway in late May 1898, the shortline progressed but slowly, for the granite slopes of the Pass proved stubborn and treacherous. Over thirty men lost their lives in construction accidents and adding to difficulties was the disappearance of workers, picks, shovels and all, whenever reports of a new find spread. With the arrival of winter came high winds, drifting snow and temperatures down to 60 below zero. Consequently, the summit of the Pass, a mere 21 miles from Skagway, was not reached until 18 February 1899. Twenty miles beyond, at Bennett, permafrost problems stymied completion for another full year. The last spike was not driven until 29 July 1900, at Carcross.

Only one rather short, 250 foot tunnel, sixteen miles from the coast, had to be bored for the entire mainline. A switchback (a hazardous zig-zag pattern of tracks with 4% grades) was needed at first to gain altitude but in 1901 it was replaced by a long steel bridge. This in turn was superseded 68 years later by a shorter bridge and tunnel but travel up and over the Pass at no time lost its awesome character, for trains continued to edge their way along narrow ledges rife with memories of mishaps past.

During the Second World War, the U.S. Army assumed operation of the railway and many extra locomotives and freight cars were brought in to handle the mountain of materials and equipment required for construction of the Alaska Highway. Control reverted to the company in May 1946 but by that time things had calmed considerably and there was no comparable boom thereafter.

Throughout the WP&Y's lifetime, all manner of life-sustaining supplies travelled inland over its rails, with virtually everything, even automobiles, containerized after 1955. Boxcars eventually disappeared from the line but tank cars managed to retain a place on the equipment register, as carriers of gasoline and aviation fuel, after a pipeline built during the war took over diesel and stove oil traffic.

Passengers, about 65,000 a year in the late 1970s, also contributed to the railway's income. Although slow (the 110 mile Whitehorse-Skagway journey took the greatest part of a day) it was the most reliable means of travel in the region. Moreover, residents and tourists alike loved the ride through what is some of the world's most spectacular and least disturbed scenery.

None of these things were enough, however, to keep the railway in business. It was the movement of bulk ore (silver, lead and zinc from the Elsa, Mayo and Faro areas, copper from around Whitehorse, and for a time asbestos from Cassiar) that made operation profitable. Widespread mine closures in 1980-81 brought hardship to the railway and by the autumn of 1982 it had to close too. When it was later disclosed that ore would be carried directly to Skagway by truck when the biggest mines reopened, the response was swift: White Pass trucks would continue to connect Vancouver and Edmonton with the Yukon but the historic and colorful rail line would be abandoned.

White Pass & Yukon's main shops, at Skagway, Alaska, built after fire destroyed the old roundhouse in 1969.

## WP & Y CHRONOLOGY

1897 — Incorporation of WP&Y constituent companies: Pacific & Arctic Rwy. & Nav. Co., B.C. Yukon Rwy. Co., and British Yukon Rwy. Co.

1898 — Construction begins; First train operating July 21st.
— Official organization of the WP&Y Rwy. Co.

1899 — White Pass summit reached Feb. 20th, Bennett July 6th.

1900 — Last Spike ceremony at Carcross July 29th.

1901 — Taku tramway (between Atlin and Tagish Lakes) incorporated into WP&Y.

1910 — Whitehorse–Pueblo copper mine spur (12 miles) built.

1918 — Pueblo branch abandoned.

1942 — Lease to U.S. Government Oct. 1st.

1946 — Control and operation returned to WP&Y Co. May 1st.

1954 — First diesels acquired.

1955 — Containerization program begun; First container ship launched.
— Riverboat service ends as Klondike Highway opens.

1964 — Last regular steam locomotive retired in June.

1969 — Skagway roundhouse burns. New shops and bulk terminal built.
— New tunnel and bridge to replace old bridge at mile 18.

1982 — Steam excursions operated June to end of August.
— Line closed.

1985 — Intention to abandon announced in October.

ABOVE: WP&Y freight behind four 1200 hp Alco/MLW diesels descends the Skagway River gorge. Over 30 men were killed building this short, 21 mile stretch to the Pass in 1898-99.

RIGHT: Tourist excursion at White Pass station (elevation 884 metres) in June, 1900. The crude, open observation car afforded unforgettable views along the cliffs during the climb. The short trip became a perennial highlight of Alaska cruise ship stopovers at Skagway, but was later made in regular parlor cars.

ABOVE: Riverboats docked at Bennett, with locomotive No. 3, a 2-8-0 of 1882 vintage on hand. Thousands of gold seekers camped here before the line was completed to Carcross and beyond at the end of July 1900, shortly after this picture was taken.

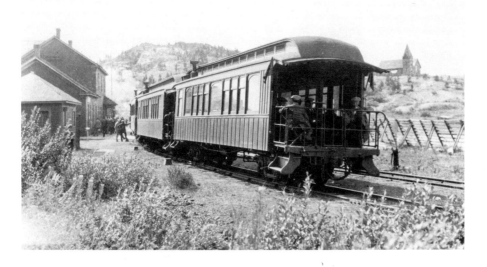

LEFT: Bennett station with a train of the 1930s. A klondike menu of beans, stew, apple pie and sourdough became traditional at this meal stop. The clerestory-roofed, open-platformed parlor cars also changed very little through the years.

ABOVE: Steam excursion behind engine number 73, on the aged wooden swing bridge at Carcross, near the spot where the last spike was driven 29 July 1900. The name Carcross is an abbreviated form of the original, "Caribou Crossing".

RIGHT: Jewel of the North, locomotive 73, building steam outside the Whitehorse engine shed. The 2-8-2 Baldwin was built in 1947 and pulled the last regular steam train on the WP&Y in June 1964. It then sat idle, on display at Bennett until being restored for excursion service in 1982.

ABOVE: Shovelnosed diesel-electrics designed for working in heavy snow conditions cross the Alaska Highway near Whitehorse. At Bennett, American crews and engines must take over for the remainder of the trip to Skagway.          BELOW: The passenger portion of the mixed train is drawn into Skagway, after the freight section had been dropped at the yards outside of town.

ABOVE: A giant straddle carrier unloading a flatcar at Whitehorse. Over 600,000 tons of freight were carried annually by the railway before closure in late 1982.

RIGHT: Flatcars with lightweight, covered ore containers wait on the Skagway terminal's sidings for the return to Whitehorse and refilling with lead-zinc concentrate.

**WHITE PASS & YUKON**

**FREIGHT EQUIPMENT**

LOWER RIGHT: WP&Y 30-foot steel caboose. Its strong vertical proportions reflect the railway's very narrow, American three foot gauge.

Sternwheel riverboat Klondike II, in service from 1936 to 1955 but now a historic monument in Whitehorse. The WP&Y operated many such vessels on the region's lakes and rivers before changing to buses and trucks.

Log-sheathed Whitehorse station exudes a frontier atmosphere, as perhaps it should. It is both the northern terminus of the White Pass & Yukon railway and the northernmost station in Canada. Company offices occupy much of the building, which has been considerably enlarged in the upper storey since it was built in 1899.

# THE GWWD RAILWAY

The Greater Winnipeg Water District Railway is western Canada's longest industrial line. Although built by the City of Winnipeg in 1913-14 for the construction and service of an aquaduct from Shoal Lake, on the Ontario border, the 97 mile railway carries out many other tasks. Freight before 1945 included firewood, lumber, poles and railway ties, ice, mail and milk. Gravel hauling to a concrete plant in St. Boniface has been a prime source of revenue in recent years and until the early 1980s, passenger service was offered.

The GWWDR has always prided itself in having good equipment. Telephone, rather than telegraph was used for train dispatching right from the start and radio traffic control was adopted as soon as that became feasible. Unlike many industrials, brand new, rather than used locomotives formed the original steam roster and when diesel-electric engines promised greater efficiency after the Second World War, they were quickly acquired.

Except in the area close to St. Boniface, relatively little agriculture could be developed along the GWWDR's route. As a result, villages along the line failed to grow. A fairly large wooden station was built at Deacon but otherwise nothing bigger than shelters was needed between St. Boniface and Indian Bay.

About midway along the line, the GWWDR enters low forest dotted with muskeg and filled with wildlife. Swallows eye the slow-moving trains from nearby hydro wires, while headstrong hawks cling to the rails, contesting right of way until the last possible moment. Game animals abound here and a few years ago a diesel was disabled in a confrontation with a moose. The engine's driver was obliged to whittle sticks to plug the badly punctured air brake tanks. Up to the time of this writing, nothing more tragic had occurred on the railway but the level crossing at the Trans-Canada Highway might be termed extremely ominous.

Apart from periodic shipments of chlorine to Waugh, very little activity now takes place on the line in winter. The warmer months are another story, for then the tiny locos move frequent trainloads of sand and gravel in addition to maintenance chores. Large projects, such as the water reservoir construction near St. Boniface in 1972 and again in 1977, which required large quantities of rock from the opposite end of the line, sometimes tax the light rail and equipment to the limit, but an unruffled calm generally pervades this most unusual little railway.

## GWWDR CHRONOLOGY

1913 — Line surveyed.
1914 — Five steam locomotives purchased.
      — Line begun, completed in December.
      — Aquaduct begun.
1919 — Aquaduct opened September 9th.
1946 — First diesel-electric locomotive acquired.
1950 — Last steam engine in operation.
1976 — Last regular passenger service. (reduced service maintained until Sept. '77).
1982 — Last summer excursions operated.

Cordwood, in great demand for heating homes before and during the great depression of the '30s, arrives at St. Boniface in 1932. Forest products, ranging from posts and poles to pulpwood for paper, were a mainstay of the GWWDR from the 1920s to '40s. Winter traffic also included considerable ice from Indian Bay in those years

THE GREATER WINNIPEG
WATER DISTRICT RAILWAY

Note: Figures in brackets are GWWDR timecard mileages from McPhillips Reservoir (Mile O), because the railway is considered part of the aquaduct. Rails actually start at Mile 5 (St. Boniface).

St. Boniface yards in 1981, with diesel 101 about to retire into the shed for the night. On the right is Mack railcar 31, originally used for passenger service but now employed only for transporting maintenance crews.

Number 7, one of four 2-6-0s bought in 1914 from Montreal Locomotive Works. An 0-4-0 saddle tank switcher and a used Mogul (2-6-0) rounded out the steam roster of the company which, incidentally, only used odd numbers on its engines. The somewhat bell-shaped emblem on cab and tender of No. 7 represents a cross-section of the aquaduct, the *raison d'être* of the line.

TOP: Baggage car 41, at St. Boniface station. Originally a Brill battery-powered railcar on the Cambrai & Indiana Railway (1916-1922) it failed to live up to expectations and was sold to the CNR, where it was converted to a simple baggage coach. The GWWD acquired it in 1935 and used it for another forty years.

LEFT: Unloading gravel at a St. Boniface concrete plant. Gravel hauling became the GWWDR's greatest revenue earner after 1945.

BELOW: End of steel at Waugh, on Indian Bay. On the left is a small brick engine shed, while to the right sits a tankcar of chlorine for Winnipeg's water supply.

# LOGGING LINES

Logging railways have always held particular fascination, for many pieces of their equipment are specialized and operations have often been bizarre. In early days their track, being temporary, was uneven and rarely well laid. Many practices were crude, not to mention unsafe. Those remaining to-day, however, are fully modern and compare very favorably with other small lines in the Canadian west.

At the very beginning, near the end of the nineteenth century, stationary steam engines, called steam donkeys, were often used to pull logs to mills or loading sites, using cables up to a mile in length. Where locomotives were used, logs were generally dragged between the rails over skid boards, which had to be sanded in wet or frosty conditions to prevent the logs from pushing the locomotives downhill. In dry weather, grease had to be applied to the skids to reduce friction. Eventually these primitive methods were replaced by the transport of logs by motor truck to rail loading areas, where proper freight cars awaited.

It was not until 1918 that government regulations obliged the use of air brakes on logging trains. Up to that time the brakes, if any, were set by hand on individual cars. Runaway trains and human injuries were commonplace, as brakemen hopped on and off, trying desperately to reset slipping gear. Link and pin couplings, another danger to workers, had to be replaced by the safer knuckle type in the 1920s, and narrow gauge, until then the preferred size of track for mountainous terrain, was likewise outlawed at this time in British Columbia, following several accidents attributed to its use.

The specialized motive power of the steam era is of particular interest. There were two main types: rod and gear drives. Rod engines often had their water tanks situated over the drive wheels rather than in tenders, for better traction. Geared locomotives were preferred, however, because of their steadier pull, greater adhesion and more accurate spotting (car positioning) capabilities. Because their exhaust was more uniform than rod engines, geared models steamed more freely, consuming less fuel, and their small diameter wheels were also a valuable asset when negotiating the uneven track, sharp curves and steep (up to 10%) grades so common to logging lines. For fire prevention, spark arrestors were fitted to engines of both categories, even when coal and oil were used as fuel, giving them a nineteenth century look.

The first steam logging railway in western Canada is believed to be one that was operated near Chemainus, on Vancouver Island, in July 1887. Hundreds of lines sprang up after that and as the timber ran out in one place, rails were moved to another, sometimes keeping the same company name, sometimes not. The development of reliable, strong motor trucks in the late 1920s gradually brought about the demise of nearly all the logging railways. Only where timber remained concentrated and where distances of transport were considereable, could rail be justified. By the 1980s, only two logging lines remained.

The forest products industry, though having generally renounced railways for logging after 1945, continued none the less to use switching locomotives at their mills. In the 1980s the impressive list of companies doing so included Abitibi Price Paper Co. (Pine Falls, Manitoba), BC Forest Products (Mackenzie and Crofton, B.C.), Canadian Cellulose (Prince Rupert, B.C.), Canadian Forest Industries (Elk Falls, B.C.), Domtar (New Westminster, B.C. and Red Rock, Ont.), Eurocan Pulp & Paper (Kitimat, B.C.), Great Lakes Pulp & Paper (Thunder Bay, Ont.), Maclean Lumber Co. (Bainbridge, B.C.), MacMillan Bloedel (Powell River, Port Alberni and Burnaby, B.C.), Minnesota Pulp & Paper (Kenora, Ont.), and Northwood Pulp & Timber (Prince George, B.C.).

The largest logging line in western Canada was the 85 mile (136 kilometre) long Abernethy Lougheed (ABOVE) operating in the hills of Maple Ridge, east of Vancouver from 1919 to 1931. Number 33, shown waiting to enter the log dump area at the junction of the Fraser and Kanaka rivers, was a Heisler gear-drive type built in 1923.

LEFT: A tiny, versatile trackmobile, economical and mobile on both track and pavement, beside Macmillan Bloedel's Burnaby plywood plant in 1984.

# THE CANFOR RAILWAY

The 63 mile long Canadian Forest products railway running south from Beaver Cove, on Vancouver Island, is the larger of the two surviving logging lines in western Canada. Trucks bring the logs to reload points along the line, where they are transferred to stake cars and drawn to Beaver Cove for sorting, grading and eventual shipment by sea to mills on the mainland. All of the railway's equipment maintenance is done at Nimpkish. Dispatching is shared between Nimpkish and Woss Camp, effectively dividing the line into three roughly equal sections.

The history of Canfor's Englewood Logging Division, which operates the railway, can be traced back to the Nimpkish Logging Company, set up in 1908 but it was not until 1917 that rails were laid to carry logs to the coast. The line was not fully complete, however, until 1957. Up to that time, there was a gap at Nimpkish Lake. Logs from the interior had to be reloaded onto barges at one end of the lake and reloaded onto freight cars again at the other, for the remaining dozen miles journey to the coast. The cost of building the missing 23 miles of railway was very high and took over three years, nine bridges and colossal amounts of blasting to complete.

Main growth of the Englewood Division began in 1944, when the Canfor Group was formed and logging rights to the Nimpkish Valley were obtained. Lines soon began to be extended and the camp/village of Woss, now so important to the railway, came into being in 1948. Vernon, at the end of the line, was established as late as 1952.

Almost every type of steam locomotive saw service on the railway, all the gear drives, and even a simple articulated 2-6-6-2 rod engine, the only one of its kind ever used in Canadian logging, trundled down its lines.

Steam locomotives of the Canfor railway began to be displaced by diesels in 1951-52, when a Shay and a Climax (gear-drive steamers) were converted to diesel power. These two engines were joined by a pair of General Motors 1200 horsepower switchers in 1956 and more were added later. The last steam engine ran in 1975.

Canfor, which has woodlands and mills in various B.C. and Alberta locations, leases over 700 flat and Thrall type boxcars to ship its products to Canadian and American markets. These brightly painted cars are possibly the only ones on the continent identifiable from the air, as will be noted in the color photo of BC Hydro's Trapp Yards on page 51.

## CANFOR RAILWAY CHRONOLOGY

1917 — Nimpkish Timber Co. builds lines.
1918 — Beaver Cove Lumber & Pulp Co. builds a railway for its pulp plant and sawmill but closes next year.
1924 — Nimpkish Timber Co. becomes the Wood & English Logging Co.
1926 — Beaver Cove Lumber & Pulp Co. assets purchased by Canadian Forest Products Ltd., a holding company of International Harvester, of Chicago.
1944 — CFP Ltd. and Wood & English Logging become the Englewood Logging Division of the Canfor Group, a Canadian company.
1957 — Missing rail link around Nimpkish Lake completed.
1975 — Last steam engine retired.

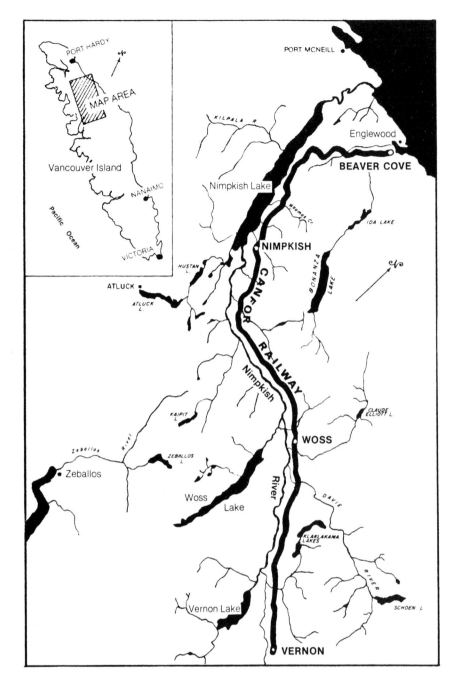

LEFT: Map of Canfor's Englewood Logging Division railway.

BELOW: Ex-Canfor 115, a three-cylinder, twelve-wheeled Pacific Coast Shay, with a tourist train at Fort Steele Historic Park, in the Kootenays. Over 2,760 Shays were built, making them the most popular of the gear-drive locomotives.

ABOVE: Locomotive 113 with a trainload of logs at a camp siding. The Alco 2-8-2 was retired in 1975, bringing steam operation on Canfor's Englewood Logging Division to an end.

Logs at the Woss reload site being transferred from truck to freight car. Trains of about 35 cars move from here to Beaver Cove.

ABOVE: Rice Creek Bridge, built in 1946 as Canfor expanded into the Nimpkish Valley. Like many timber trestles, it was later filled in with earth to remove the possibility of destruction by fire.

LEFT: A husky, steel-jawed stacker removes logs from a flatcar at the Beaver Cove dryland sort area.

# THE CFI RAILWAY

The Crown Forest Industries railway, between the Nanaimo Lakes and Ladysmith, B.C., is a fairly simple operation. A log sort and load facility sits at one end, a seaside unload area and small yards at the other, with no stations or camps in between. Traffic control on the approximately 20 mile line is by radio from the Ladysmith maintenance sheds. Train crews consist of only three men: a driver, a conductor and a brakeman, about a third of the number required in the steam era.

Origins of the CFI railway lie in the formation in 1909 of the Comox & Campbell Lake Tramway Company, reorganized in 1910 as the Comox Logging & Railway Company. Numerous lines were built through forested lands in the Courtenay-Comox region, their extent varying between 50 and 75 miles as rails were moved to follow timber harvesting. In 1943, the Comox L&R Co. built a line from Ladysmith to the Nanaimo Lakes and moved some of its equipment to that area. Ten years later, when the company was sold, the Headquarters operation was closed down, leaving rail activity restricted to the Nanaimo Lakes line.

For the next thirty years, the Nanaimo Lakes line functioned as part of Crown Zeller-bach Canada Ltd., and was dieselized in the early 1960s. In 1983, the railway again changed hands, this time becoming part of Crown Forest Industries Limited, a subsidiary of Fletcher Challenge, a multinational corporation with headquarters in New Zealand.

With the purchase of Crown Zellerbach Canada, CFI also came into possession of the Elk Falls pulp and paper mill, near Campbell River, midway up the east coast of Vancouver Island. There an ageing, 1943 model 1,000 h.p. Baldwin that in 1960 began dieselization of the Nanaimo Lakes line, was said to be still doing switching as of this writing.

## CFI RAILWAY CHRONOLOGY

1909 — Comox & Campbell Lake Tramway Co., a subsidiary of Fraser River Lumber Co. formed.
1910 — Fraser River Lumber reincorporates as the Canadian Western Lumber Co. and renames the C&CL Tramway the Comox Logging & Railway Co.
1943 — Nanaimo Lakes line built by Comox L&R Co.
1950 — Canadian Western Lumber becomes joint owner with Pacific Mills of the Elk Falls pulp and paper mill.
1953 — Crown Zellerbach takes over Pacific Mills, Canadian Western and the Comox L&R Co., whose Headquarters operation is shut down and equipment moved to the Nanaimo Lakes line.
1960 — Dieselization begun.
1962 — Last steam engine, No. 11, retired (see color photo page 54).
1983 — CZ Canada becomes Crown Forest Industries October 1st.

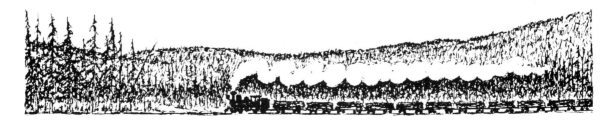

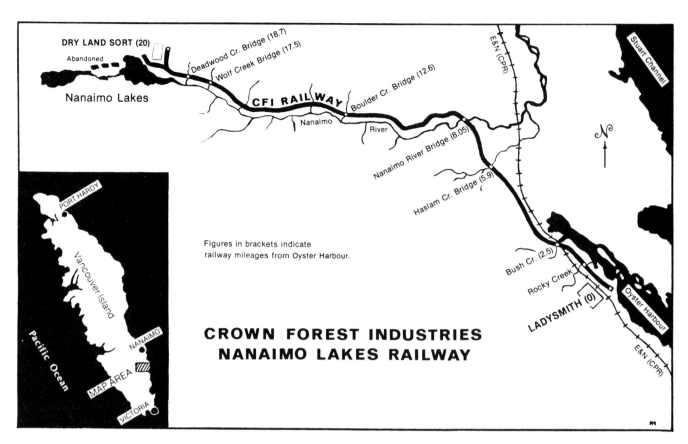

DRY LAND SORT (20)

Abandoned

Nanaimo Lakes

Deadwood Cr. Bridge (18.7)

Wolf Creek Bridge (17.5)

CFI RAILWAY

Boulder Cr. Bridge (12.6)

Nanaimo

River

Nanaimo River Bridge (8.05)

Haslam Cr. Bridge (5.9)

E&N (CPR)

Stuart Channel

Figures in brackets indicate
railway mileages from Oyster Harbour.

Bush Cr. (2.5)

Rocky Creek

LADYSMITH (0)

Oyster Harbour

E&N (CPR)

PORT HARDY

Vancouver Island

Pacific Ocean

NANAIMO

MAP AREA

VICTORIA

## CROWN FOREST INDUSTRIES
## NANAIMO LAKES RAILWAY

Bundled logs being unloaded at Ladysmith. A crane will later lift them from the water onto barges
for shipment to mills elsewhere.

Ladysmith engine and maintenance sheds, with CFI diesel 8427 (an ex-CPR locomotive) at right and 4097 (a hybrid of two ex-Delaware & Hudson locos) at left. Both are Alco RS-3s of the 1950s.

Modern steel log cars of the Crown Forest Industries railway. Their hinged staves can swing down for simple unloading. Earlier models had wooden frames with staves that had to be loosened by hand. The logs then tumbled off as the cars were drawn over tracks with one rail higher than the other.

CFI log train, headed by a water sprinkler car, crossing a timber trestle on the Nanaimo Lakes line. Heat and sparks from wheels made smoking hot from constant downhill braking pose a serious threat to the wooden bridges and surrounding forest in dry weather.

CFI Firefighting and maintenance crews can be moved quickly in self-propelled speeders like this one amid the verdant Nanaimo Lakes landscape.

# OTHER INDUSTRIALS

Most industrial railways in western Canada are short, often consisting of not more than a mile or so of track and an engine or two, but all are important to the general well being of both the companies who own them and the continental rail network. They are particularly practical and economical in that freight cars can be moved to synchronize exactly with production schedules, greatly reducing delays and improving overall efficiency.

Motive power for the industrials tends to be small, for normally only a few cars are moved at any one time. To-day, diesel and diesel-electrics predominate but a few propane and straight electric locomotives may also be found. Some are especially designed for certain tasks but a large number of them have traditionally been bought second-hand from the big railways, after they were found to be too light, old, or underpowered for regular service there. One valuable side effect of this practice has been the saving of some historically important locomotives from untimely demise at the salvage yard. Perhaps the most famous case was that of the Countess of Dufferin, the Canadian Pacific's first engine, which spent many of its late years in Golden, B.C. serving a lumber company, before being rescued for preservation at Winnipeg.

Private freight cars are another interesting aspect of industrial railroading. Some cars, such as ore dumpers, slag carriers, etc., never leave plant premises. Others, such as Sultran Corporation's nearly 700 gondolas, are expressly for service on the regular railways. These cars are inevitabley large, designed for economical transport of basic commodities such as sulphur, potash and lumber, to coastal terminals and distant markets. In spite of the company names painted on the sides, however, many are merely leased, not owned.

## Mining and Smelting

Railway transport has been almost indispensable to the mining industry for a very long time. The low friction of steel against steel is ideal for moving heavy loads such as ore, and when flanges are added to the wheels, trains can follow confined underground routes with ease. An old German mining textbook of 1530 showed plankways already in use and railways were introduced at the Newcastle on Tyne coalfields in England in 1602. Two centuries later, the first steam locomotive to run on rails was built by Richard Trevithick and demonstrated at the Pen-y-Darren Colliery and Iron Works at Dowlais.

It is not too astonishing then, that the first full-fledged, steam-powered railway in western Canada was built to haul coal, from mines of the Vancouver Coal Mining & Land Co. in the Nanaimo area, down to the harbour in 1863. Its first locomotive, an 0-4-0 named **Pioneer**, had to be brought around Cape Horn from England, for neither a transcontinental railroad nor a Panama Canal yet existed.

Several mining companies to-day still use rail for short surface hauls, for example the six-mile line of the Bienfait Coal Co., in southeastern Saskatchewan. On the other hand, underground mining by rail has declined significantly in recent years, although it can be found at places like Kimberley, B.C. There are several attractive alternatives, such as open pit mining with draglines and giant motor trucks, or sectional conveyor belts like those at Sylvite of Canada's Rocanville, Sask. potash mine, which can be extended up to 4,000 feet. Rail has thus become less and less inseparable from mining as the 20th century progressed.

Fireless locomotives for underground mining at Coleman, in southwestern Alberta, about 1912. Air at 500 pounds pressure was put into their tanks, enough for a round trip below. These and electric machines replaced the less sanitary, less productive mules and horses of earlier times. Note the crude track curvature at the turnout, so characteristic of mine railways, whose equipment was generally very short and rudimentary.

Smelting, which involves the movement of heavy and often molten materials, continues to require railways at the largest plants. These include the Aluminum Co. of Canada at Kitimat, Cominco Ltd. at Trail, B.C., and Hudson Bay Mining & Smelting at Flin Flon, Manitoba.

### Grain

While the big railways do the long distance hauling of grain and shunt cars at prairie elevators, they seldom handle switching at terminal points. The numerous grain companies that prefer to have their own locomotives include the Saskatchewan Wheat Pool, Cargill and Pioneer Grain at Thunder Bay, Ontario, Prince Rupert Grain Ltd. at Prince Rupert, United Grain Growers and Pacific Elevators at Vancouver, and Pioneer Grain at North Vancouver, B.C. In addition, a hook and cable system is used at some elevators, such as the Saskatchewan Wheat Pool in N. Vancouver, to reduce dependancy on the regular railways.

The list of other industries with their own private lines is long and varied. It includes sugar refineries, oil and chemical plants, cement, iron and steel works, fertilzer companies, electric power generating stations, certain construction firms, and port terminals at Churchill, Manitoba, N. Vancouver and Victoria, B.C. Altogether, there were over 75 industrial railways in western Canada in 1985 and if put together they would make a very formidable railroad indeed.

RIGHT: Unloading grain from a boxcar at a coastal elevator. Gripped by the couplers, the car is tilted and rocked to empty grain through the open side door. Before this hydraulic machinery was developed in 1920 for the CNR elevator at Port Arthur, wooden inner door barriers were removed with axes and chain-drawn shovels were used to clear out the grain.

**The Crow Rate**
Grain was long unprofitable to carry in western Canada because of the **Crow's Nest Agreement** of 1897. Originally signed by the CPR in return for land grants and subsidies to build the Lethbridge-Nelson line, Crow was to have applied only to common grains shipped to the lakehead and only to the Canadian Pacific Railway. Political pressure extended it to the CNR, then to westbound export grain (in 1927) and finally to northbound shipments to Churchill (1931). While farmers saved money on the low rates, the railways fared poorly. Government grain cars were necessary by 1972 and the Crow Rate was belatedly abolished at the end of 1983.

BELOW: Dwarfed by their mammoth loads, Plymouth industrial switchers shunt 100-ton, easily unloaded covered hoppers at the Pioneer Grain Company's North Vancouver terminal elevator.

ABOVE: Vancouver Wharves locomotive 21 gingerly handling methanol tank cars from Alberta. Sulphur, ore, sand and other bulk materials are also handled at this busy oceanside terminal.

BELOW: Potash and lumber cars of private companies awaiting customs clearance at Huntingdon, B.C. before continuing south to the United States.

# RAPID TRANSIT

The term Rapid Transit has been in use for over a century and was once broadly applied not only to elevated and subway systems but also to their lighter cousins, the street railways. Movement through urban centres was generally faster by any of these means than by other conveyances of the horse and buggy era. Only in the 1920s, when the majority of North American streets had become paved and motor vehicles numerous enough to seriously obstruct streetcar movement, did application of the term narrow to mean only high speed systems running exclusively, or nearly exclusively on their own, private rights-of-way.

Rapid Transit began with London, England's Metropolitan Line, opened in 1863. Essentially an underground, it escaped from the tangle of surface traffic above it. Cost of constructing systems of this sort has always been extremely high, requiring very densely populated areas to sustain them. Consequently, few of them have been built and Canada did not see one until Toronto's came into being in 1954.

A practical, though admittedly inferior substitute, was a streetcar network. Travel was slower but expensive tunneling, with all its problems of rock and water, could be eliminated and the lighter equipment was considerably cheaper. For these reasons, Canadian municipalities did not hesitate to chose them, putting off the question of true rapid transit until some unspecified date in the future.

As of this writing, Winnipeg had neither a modern rapid transit system nor plans to build one, yet it was there, in 1882, that the first street railway in western Canada was built. Its cars were horsedrawn but the horsecar era was shortlived, for the animals were slow and could only do five hours of work per day. They disappeared in short order when electric trams arrived. Both Victoria and Vancouver opened electric systems in 1890 and Winnipeg converted the following year.

City dwellers were happy to overcome abominable muddy road conditions with their new streetcars but as the years went on serious flaws began to emerge. Automobile and cycle riders hated the bumps and tracking caused by rails set in bricks in the middle of the streets and streetcar passengers faced a growing hazard at stops, where they had to cross the paths of motor vehicles.

Resistance of labor unions to one-man operated trams, the relative cheapness of petroleum and the concerted effort of certain automotive, oil and tire interests to convert systems to bus operation further added to the decline and fall of the streetcar. By the end of the 1950s, every single one of the many streetcar networks in western Canada had been replaced by rubber-tired vehicles.

For awhile, rapid transit appeared to be a dead issue but as oil-fuelled vehicles proliferated their disadvantages became all too apparent. Traffic congestion, poisonous fumes and an insufferable noise were seen to place human health in jeopardy. Freeway construction solved none of these problems. Moreover, they were enormously costly, their waste of valuable land intolerable.

By the end of the 1960s, the Rapid Transit idea had once again come to life in western Canada. A double track could carry the equivalent of eleven lanes of freeway, with none of its pollution, and while streetcars were briefly reconsidered they were found wanting in speed. Fast, technologically advanced urban trains promised much better solutions to the problems and plans for such systems soon began to be laid.

Single-truck electric tram at the Esquimalt Canteen Grounds, in 1898. On this route, sailors sometimes helped rerail cars that had jumped the tracks, a none too rare occurrence with these tipsy four-wheelers. Having cabs at both ends, they did not need to be wyed at the end of the run. The conductor merely reversed the trolley pole and the motorman took his controller handle to the other end of the car.

LEFT: Sweeper cars at Kitsilano yards in Vancouver, January 1924. Snow, ice, fallen leaves and other debris on the tracks were quickly removed by the rotating brushes of these effective, albeit awkward looking machines, and even the smallest street railway owned at least one of them.

Early Vancouver trams driving on the left, English fashion. When the Rule of the Road was changed, on 1 January 1922, doors had to be placed on the other side, turnouts and overhead wiring reversed in a round-the-clock, overnight operation. Streetcars would then rumble and clang amongst these solid stone buildings for another 33 years.

Sightseeing in special, open trolleys was offered by many street railways in Canada. This observation car toured Vancouver for two hours, while conductor Teddy Lyons amused passengers with anecdotes and witty comments. Date of the photo is 1929.

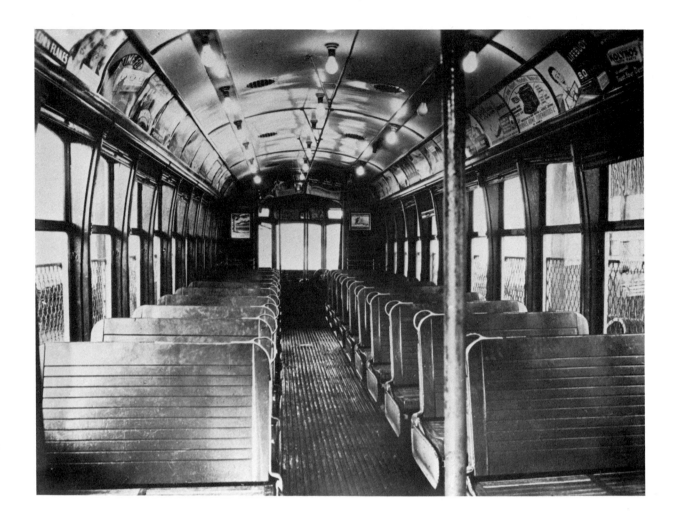

STREET RAILWAYS AND INTERURBANS IN WESTERN CANADA
AT THE HEIGHT OF THE FIRST RAPID TRANSIT ERA, (1914).

| Company | Mileage |
|---|---|
| Brandon Municipal Rwy. | 8.5 |
| B.C. Electric Rwy. | 241.9 |
| Calgary Municipal Rwy. | 55.0 |
| Edmonton Interurban Rwy. | 8.2 |
| Edmonton Radial Rwy. | 50.5 |
| Fort William Electric Rwy. | 11.6 |
| Lethbridge Municipal Rwy. | 11.0 |
| Moose Jaw Electric Rwy. | 9.0 |
| Nelson Street Rwy. | 2.1 |
| Port Arthur Electric Rwy. | 12.4 |
| Regina Municipal Rwy. | 30.8 |
| Saskatoon Municipal Rwy. | 12.6 |
| Winnipeg Electric Rwy. | 100.9 |
| Winnipeg, Selkirk & Lake Winnipeg Rwy. | 22.1 |

Notes:
1. Both Estevan, Sask. and Medicine Hat, Alta. were projecting street railways at this time.
2. The Mount McKay & Kakabeka Falls Rwy., which was projected as an interurban line from Fort William to the Falls, only grew to be a five mile long gravel carrier.

ABOVE: The interior of a pre-1930 streetcar. Its reversible, wood slat seats, antislip floors, advertising cards and wire window grilles were typical for Canada. The generous, comfortable width was never matched by buses.

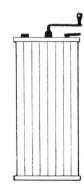

ABOVE: Two of Nelson, B.C.'s three streetcars on Front Street, about 1940. With barely two miles of track, it was Canada's smallest tram system, but it gave valued service for half a century, 1899 to 1949.

BELOW: Calgary's last streetcar, 29 December 1950. The McCauley door on the tram's front corner was a safety feature, allowing the motorman a better view of boarding passengers. These cars also had a hole in the floor, through which the driver could line switches with an iron bar, saving both time and inconvenience.

**Streetcars To Meet Road Competition:** Edmonton's 51-seat cars of 1930 (ABOVE), built by the Ottawa Car Co., boasted leather upholstery, storm windows, and one-man operation. Fast, quiet, standardized PCC cars (BELOW) had both air and magnetic track brakes. Under a President's Conference Committee, North American street railways organized its development in 1929 and by 1934 the first model emerged from the St. Louis Car Co. While Vancouver bought several between 1938 and 1945, they were discarded with the rest of the West's trams in the 1950s.

# EDMONTON LRT

While Heavy Rapid Transit (HRT), built essentially underground and equipped with large coaches, had been selected for Toronto and Montreal, it was not found entirely appropriate for western Canadian cities, where populations were smaller and less concentrated. Light Rapid Transit (LRT) was not only more attractive cost-wise, it had been proven effective abroad for many years. In the United States, slightly modified PCC streetcars had successfully run in trains of several units over private rights-of-way in Cleveland and Boston since the early 1960s. More advanced systems had been developed in Europe, notably Germany, where S-bahns (Schnellbahns) were proliferating. They had been aided by heavy federal funding because of the recognition of their equal importance with highways. One other German urban transit development, the monorail, vied for Canadian consideration but because of its inherant difficulty of maintenance and accessibility received only minor attention.

After having discarded the idea of reintroducing streetcars, Edmonton led the rebirth of Rapid Transit in western Canada with the building of a 600 volt D.C. electric railway, opened in 1978. The line connected the northeast portion of the city with the Exhibition Grounds, the Colosseum, and the downtown core. Subsequent extensions have taken rails to Clareview, on the city's northern outskirts, and to the Provincial Legislative Buildings, west of the original terminus at Central Station.

The Edmonton system is essentially a surface route, with some streets overpassed, others protected by automatic crossing gates. Only as the line approaches the downtown area from the north at 95th Street does it descend into underground tunnel, turning westward at Central Station to run beneath Jasper Avenue for about a mile toward the Alberta Parliament.

Continuous welded steel rail is used throughout the system and travel in the insulated and rubber-suspensioned cars is very smooth and quiet. Coach seats are wool upholstered (especially welcome in a cold climate) and both heating and ventilating are adequate. All units to date have been Siemens-Duwag articulated double coaches, open full width through the central hinge area to make movement easy from end to end.

Stations on the Edmonton LRT are not elaborate in design but are well lit and decorated in cheerful, light colors. To reduce noise, rubber matting and rock ballast were positioned between the tracks and their concrete support slabs. Most stations are single level but Central and Churchill have two: one for train platforms, the other for shops and ticket dispensing. A proof of purchase system is in use, with time-marked tickets that must be kept by the passenger for inspection at any time. Fines are levied for invalid tickets. The method eliminates the need for separate entrances and exits at stations and has a speeding effect on passenger flow. Station security is enhanced by the use of closed circuit television, in operation day and night.

When extensions to the Edmonton LRT make direct connections with important public centres like the university and the airport, the full potential of the system will be realized. Meanwhile, its function as an express adjunct to the bus network has already proved successful. A steady growth pattern developed from the very beginning and by the early 1980s ridership had risen to over six million passengers annually.

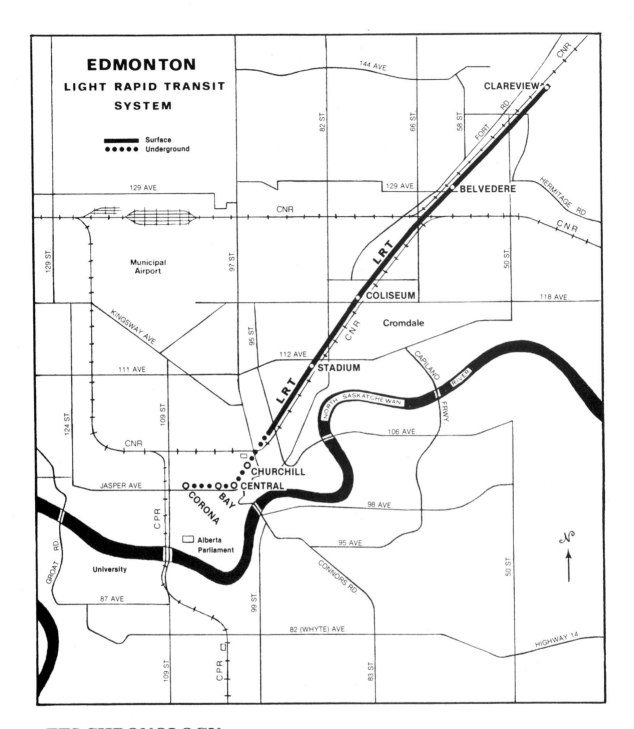

## ETS CHRONOLOGY

1908 — Edmonton Radial Rwy. opens Nov. 9th (on Jasper Ave.).

1932 — First bus introduced (on 102 Ave.).

1939 — Electric trolley busses introduced.

1946 — Name changed to Edmonton Transportation System.

1947 — Name changed to Edmonton Transit System.

1951 — Last streetcar operates Sept. 2nd (on 109 Street).

1961 — Reintroduction of streetcars proposed.

1973 — Approval for an LRT given.

1974 — Construction begins on LRT.

1978 — LRT opened April 23rd.

1981 — Clareview extension opened April 26th.

1983 — Extension to Parliament opened in June.

A four car Edmonton Transit train passing the Cromdale LRT shops. These Siemens/Duwag units are equipped with high-speed pantographs, which eliminate the de-wiring problems associated with trolley poles.

ETS work locomotive 2001, under repair at the Cromdale shops. A true boomer, it was built in 1912 by Alco/General Electric for the Oregon Electric Railway (number 21), sold to the BC Electric in 1946 (No. 961), then resold to Edmonton in 1980, where it was put to work at construction and maintenance tasks.

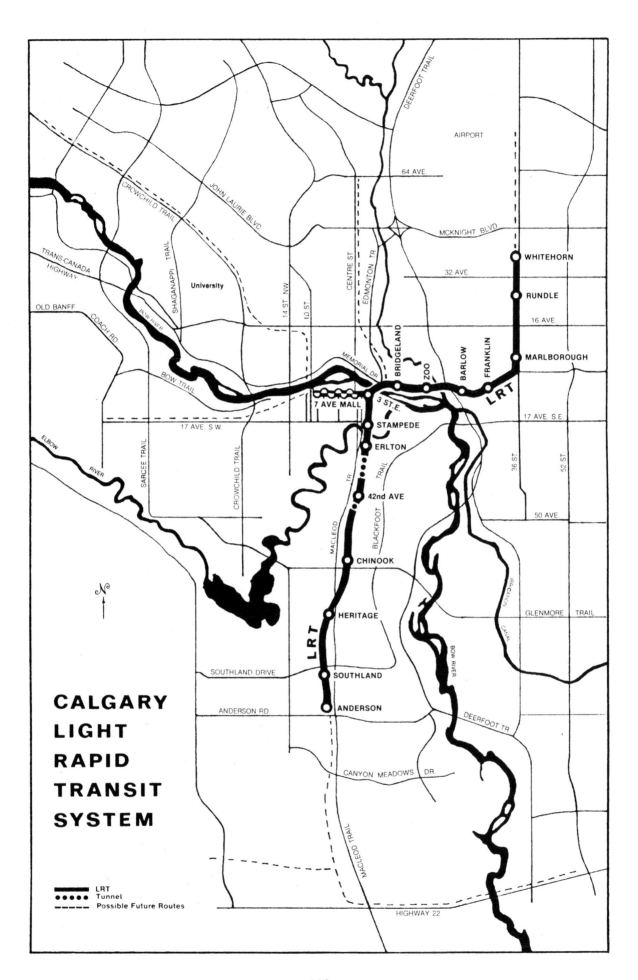

# CALGARY LIGHT RAPID TRANSIT SYSTEM

Legend:
- LRT
- Tunnel
- Possible Future Routes

# CALGARY LRT

To speed crosstown travel and alleviate downtown traffic congestion, Calgary began building a Light Rapid Transit system in May, 1978. Three years later the first section, 7.7 miles long, from Anderson Road north to Seventh Avenue and west to between Eighth and Ninth Streets West, was duly opened.

From Anderson to 42nd Avenue South, the line follows the Canadian Pacific's right-of-way, then continues on its own, tunnels under Cemetery Hill, skirts the Stampede Grounds, then dives under the CPR mainline to reach Seventh Avenue. A bridge over the Elbow River represented the only other construction feature of note to this point.

The Seventh Avenue portion of the system is unique in Canadian rapid transit. The street is closed to all but transit trains and busses. Intersections with cross streets are controlled by regular traffic lights. Grooved rails set into the pavement give a streetcar-like appearance to the operation here but the continuous welded rail and high, convenient loading platforms set it well apart from tramlines of old.

In 1984, an expansion program saw rails laid from 7th Avenue at 3rd Street East to the other side of the Bow River, via a new bridge. The line was then run eastward, along the median of Memorial Drive to 36 Street East, where it turned northward to Whitehorn Station, at 39th Avenue N.E. A short tunnel and some overpasses freed the LRT from major level crossings.

Calgary chose Siemens-Duwag articulated U2 coaches, similar to those acquired by Edmonton Transit. In addition to an established reputation for comfort and dependability, these units offered built in heated sanders and electronic anti-slip devices for winter operation. They also contained many desirable safety features. The train's driver is in constant radio contact with a central dispatcher and lights in the cab warn of other trains in the signal block ahead. Coach doors open only after release by a switch in the cab and pressure sensitive door edges guard against premature closure on passengers.

Use of C-Trains (C for Calgary or Cummuter) is encouraged by providing free electric plug-ins for automobile blockheaters at some suburban stations. Transfers are valid on bus or LRT and downtown travel within Seventh Avenue is free of charge. Train frequency at rush hours is every five minutes, so travel to the downtown area by any other means can seldom be justified. Studies made since LRT construction indicate that up to half of automobile commuters have indeed switched to the trains. Further extension of the system to other parts of the city will no doubt reduce road traffic even more, meeting all the original objectives of the rapid transit scheme.

## CTS CHRONOLOGY

1909 — Calgary Municipal Rwy. opens (from Victoria Park to First St. West).
1932 — First busses (on Mount Royal route).
1947 — First trolley busses (Crescent Heights route).
1948 — Name changes to Calgary Transit System.
1950 — Last streetcar operates December 29th (on Ogden route).
1978 — Construction of LRT begins.
1981 — LRT opens May 25th, Anderson to Seventh Avenue.
1985 — Northeast extension complete.

Open House at Calgary Transit's Anderson Shops, where new Siemens/Duwag U2 coaches are being assembled. These vehicles, of German design, feature welded steel bodies, electronic anti-slip devices and rubber wheel inserts for quieter operation. As can be seen in the diagram below, they work in articulated pairs, with a shared bogie under the hinge area. Operating current is 600 volts direct current. Maximum speed: 50 mph (80 km/hr).

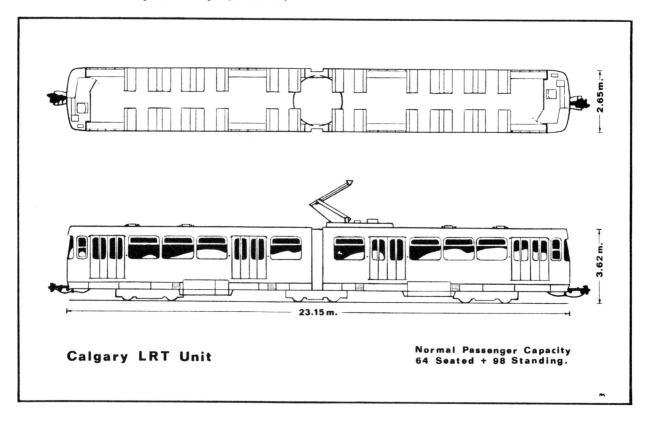

2.65 m.

3.62 m.

23.15 m.

**Calgary LRT Unit**

**Normal Passenger Capacity
64 Seated + 98 Standing.**

# VANCOUVER REGIONAL ALRT

Although Vancouver had excellent rail transit from an early date, provided by the BC Electric, it was given up in the 1950s. Two-car tram trains and modern PCC cars had proven only partially effective in the growing city traffic. Movement through the metropolis averaged only about seven miles per hour at times. Private right-of-way existed solely for interurbans and even they had to use city streets for part of their runs.

After much debate, the province announced in 1978 the formation of an Urban Transit Authority and shortly thereafter embarked upon a bold, completely new course. On 1 March 1982, Phase One of the Vancouver Regional Rapid Transit system, between downtown Vancouver and New Westminster (21.4 km) was begun. Less than four years later, on 3 January 1986, it was officially in operation. Its advanced design incorporated the largest application of linear induction technology in the world. It would be a showpiece of Canadian transportation expertise during the world Exposition held later that year in Vancouver.

The coaches, designed and built by the Urban Transportation Development Corporation of Ontario, move by exerting electromagnetic force on a wide central rail, which acts in effect as a stator. Because wheels support and steer but do not propel the vehicles, adhesion problems are eliminated. Icy conditions are of no consequence and grades of up to 8% present little difficulty. Other features include axles that move to face wheels into curves, reducing noise and wear, and gearless motors that contain no moving parts whatever. Aluminum and fibreglass coach bodies ensure long life and minimum maintenance elsewhere.

Unlike the Edmonton and Calgary systems, the Vancouver ALRT (A for Advanced or Automated) was designed for driverless, computer controlled operation. To accomplish this safely, the system has no level crossings. All roads pass either under or over the rail line. In downtown Vancouver, the ALRT runs underground, using the ex-CPR Dunsmuir tunnel from False Creek to the Burrard Inlet waterfront. Most of the remainder of the system is elevated on concrete guideways, following in large part the Central Park line of the BC Hydro Railway to New Westminster.

Station design, by various Vancouver architects, was heavily influenced by the Architektengruppe U-Bahn of Vienna, whose standardization and modular approach offered sound solutions to building and maintenance problems. Considerable amounts of glass and glossy tile in the structures give a feeling of light and airyness (making the system's nickname "Skytrain" quite apt) and tubular steel used to support canopies of surface stations seems to add to an overall freedom and fluidity. Long platforms, level with coach floors, accommodate trains up to eight cars in length and like other transit systems' they have video security surveillance. Convenience is heightened by the provision of escalators and elevators to supplement stairs at some stops.

The VRRT cuts crosstown travel time to a fraction of that required by other surface vehicles. It connects with North Vancouver via the Seabus terminal (the former CPR station) at the foot of Granville street, and extensions to the other end, beyond New Westminster, are designed to attract ridership from Surrey and Port Coquitlam. Response to the attractive system was favorable from the outset and it is likely that extensions will eventually link the entire Greater Vancouver area.

# VRRT CHRONOLOGY

1890 — Vancouver Street Rwy. Co. opens (on Main and Cordova Sts.).
1891 — Central Park Line opens in October (Westminster & Vancouver Tramway Co.).
1897 — BC Electric Co. forms, absorbing Vancouver Street Rwy. and the Westminster & Vancouver Tramway.
1922 — Rule of Road changes from left to right January 1st.
1923 — First bus in Vancouver (on Grandview).
1924 — BC Rapid Transit, a private truck and bus company, forms.
1932 — BC Rapid Transit Co. taken over by BC Electric Co.
1948 — First trolleybusses Aug. 16th (Fraser, Davie, Robson lines).
1954 — Central Park Line interurbans discontinued.
1955 — Last streetcar in Vancouver April 24th.
1961 — BC Electric Co. becomes Provincially-owned BC Hydro.
1972 — Streetcars reconsidered.
1978 — Urban Transit Authority formed.
1980 — Metro Transit Operating Co. formed to operate Vancouver and Victoria transit systems.
1982 — Sod turned for new ALRT March 1st.
1983 — UTA becomes BC Transit.
       — ALRT demonstration/test section opens on Terminal Ave.
1985 — MTOC absorbed by BC Transit in June.
       — ALRT complete Vancouver to New Westminster in November.
1986 — Regular service on ALRT begins January 3rd.

Demonstration train approaching the Main Street Station, in 1983. The fully automated system is mostly elevated on concrete guideways to avoid level crossings. Vertical columns were cast in place at hundred foot intervals, then the long horizontal beams, precast in a Richmond plant, were trucked to the site and hoisted into position.

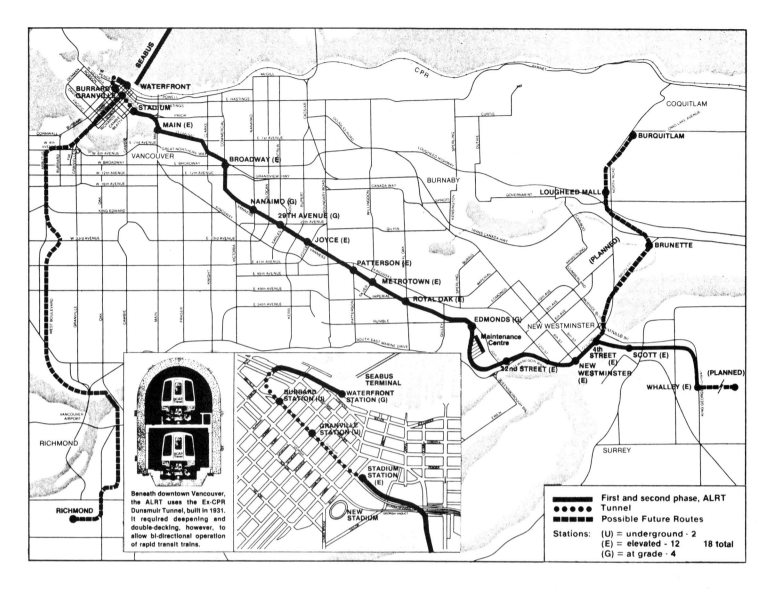

Beneath downtown Vancouver, the ALRT uses the Ex-CPR Dunsmuir Tunnel, built in 1931. It required deepening and double-decking, however, to allow bi-directional operation of rapid transit trains.

| | |
|---|---|
| ━━━━━ | First and second phase, ALRT |
| ●●●●● | Tunnel |
| ■■■■■ | Possible Future Routes |

Stations: (U) = underground · 2
(E) = elevated · 12   18 total
(G) = at grade · 4

The Vancouver cars obtain their electric power from a steel-capped, aluminum third rail mounted on the inner side of the guideway. Current is the same as that of the Edmonton and Calgary systems (600 volts d.c.) but it is converted to three-phase a.c. on board the Vancouver coaches, for performance reasons. The linear induction units take the many steep grades on the VRRT with ease. This one is at Edmonds Station, in Burnaby.

117

# INDEX

Bold Italics indicate photographs

| | |
|---|---|
| Abbotsford | 67 |
| Abernethy Lougheed | *90* |
| Alaska | 76-83 |
| Alberta Govt. | 43 |
| Alberta & Great Waterways | 43 |
| Alberta Midland | 31 |
| Alberta Pioneer Rail Ass'n. | 35,*45* |
| Alberta Resources Rwy. | 29,31,42 |
| Alberta Wheat Pool | *22* |
| Aluminum | 100,115,117 |
| Amtrak | 47 |
| Annacis Island | *74* |
| Arbutus Canyon | *28* |
| Armstrong, Ont. | 29 |
| Articulated Equipment | *39*,91,109,*114* |
| Auto Racks | 16,*74* |
| Avalanches | 7,15 |
| Banff | *9*,*17* |
| Barrhead | 43 |
| Basque, B.C. | 31 |
| Beaver Cove | 91 |
| Beavers | 9,11 |
| Bennett, B.C. | 77,*80*,82 |
| Bienfait | 99 |
| Biggar | 29 |
| Blaine | 47 |
| Blue River | *36* |
| Boston | 109 |
| Boxcars | 72,77,91,*101* |
| Brakes | 41,89,108 |
| Brandon | 47 |
| Bridges | *6*,*21*,*22*,*25*,*28*,*40*,*54*,*70*,*81*,*94*,*98* |
| British Columbia Hydro Rwy. | *51*,66-75, *111*,115 |
| British Columbia Rwy. | 29,43,*51*,57-65 |
| Burlington Northern | 10,47-48,57,67,70 |
| Burnaby | 30,31,68,*90*,117 |
| Burrard Inlet | 23 |
| Byron Creek | *21* |
| Cabooses | *22*,*41*,*46*,*63*,*72*,*75*,*83* |
| Calgary | 9,11,14,17,18,31,*55*,*107*,112-114 |
| Cambrai & Indiana | 88 |
| Campbell River | 23 |
| Canadian | *2*,*19* |
| Canadian Forest Products | *54*,91-94 |
| Canadian Govt. Rwys. | 29,31 |
| Canadian National Rwys. | 29-46,47,*50*, 57,*65*,67,70 |
| Canadian Northern Rwy. | 29,31,35 |
| Canadian Pacific Rwy. | *2*,*6*,*8*,*9*-28,29, 43,47,*49*,57,67,113 |
| Carberry | 31 |
| Carcross | 77,*81* |
| Central Canada Rwy. | 43 |
| Central Traffic Control | 9,25 |
| Centralized Agencies | 25 |
| Chemainus | 89 |
| Chilliwack | 67 |
| Chipmunk | 57 |
| Churchill | 29,31,39 |
| Cleveland | 109 |
| Cliffside | 23 |
| Clover Bar | *40* |
| Cloverdale | 40,48,57 |
| Coal | 9,30,*40*,47,57,*65*,99 |
| Coleman | *100* |
| Colonist Coaches | 7 |
| Columbia & Western | 11 |
| Comox | 23,*54* |
| Computers | 9,115 |
| Concrete Ties | 30,31 |
| Confederation | 10,11,23 |
| Connaught | 2,16,71 |
| Containers | 49,77,83 |
| Coquihalla | 11 |
| Coughlin | 71 |
| Countess of Dufferin | 99 |
| Couplings | *65*,89 |
| Courtenay | 23 |
| Coutts - Sweetgrass | 47 |
| Cowichan Lake | 23,*26* |
| Craigellachie | 11 |
| Crews | 35,61,63,74,95,*104* |
| Crocker, C. | 23 |
| Crow Rate | 11,30,101 |
| Crow's Nest | 6,10,11,20,47 |
| Crown Forest Industries | 95-98 |
| Current Collection | 104,111,118 |
| Dawson Creek | 43 |
| Dease Lake | 57 |
| Deep Bay | 67,69 |
| Dieselization | 8,11,24,27,31,44,53,62,67,95 |
| Double Tracking | 9,30 |
| Dunsmuir | 23 |
| Dunvegan Yards | 44 |
| Edmonton | 11,18,29,31,*34*,43,*44*,55, 77,*108*,109-111 |
| Electric Operation | 8,30,*51*,55,57, 67-73,103-118 |
| Elk Falls | 95 |
| Elko | 47 |
| Emerson | 10,11,31 |
| Englewood | 91,93 |
| Esquimalt | *24*,*104* |
| Esquimalt & Nanaimo Rwy. | 11,23-28,*49* |
| Female Conductors | 75 |
| Fernie | 47 |
| Ferries | *41*,*49*,57 |
| Fibreglass | 115 |
| Field | 11,14 |
| Firefighting | *9*,*98* |
| Fireless Locos | *100* |
| Fleming, Sandford | 10,11 |
| Flin Flon | 100 |
| Foley, Welch & Stewart | 57 |
| Forest Products | 27,30,47,*54*,57,64,67, 85,86,89-98,*102* |
| Fort Fraser | 31 |
| Fort MacMurray | 43 |
| Fort Nelson | 57 |
| Fort St. James | 57 |
| Fort St. John | 57 |
| Fort Steele | *92* |
| Fort William | *18* |
| Fraser | *38*,67,*70*,90 |
| Freeways | 103 |
| Gear Drive | 89,90-92 |
| Golden | 99 |
| Goldstream | *25* |
| Grades | 14,16,67,89,115,*117* |
| Grain | 9,10,*22*,30,*39*,49,53,100,*101* |
| Grand Cache | 42 |
| Grand Prairie | 42 |
| Grand Trunk | 29,30,31 |
| Grand Trunk Pacific | 18,29,31,*36*,*40* |
| Gravel | 85,*88* |
| Great Central | 23 |
| Great Northern — see Burlington Northern | |
| Great Slave Lake | 29,42,43 |
| GWWD Rwy. | *53*,85-88 |
| Hay River | 29,42 |
| Hector | 11 |
| Helicopters | 9 |
| Henry, M.J. | 77 |
| Hill, J.J. | 10,11,47 |
| Horne-Payne, R. | 67 |
| Horse Train | 7 |
| Hot Box Detector | *16* |
| Howe Sound | 58,60 |
| Hudson Bay | 29,31,*34*,47 |
| Hudson Locos | *17*,58 |
| Huntingdon | 11,47,67,*75*,*102* |
| Huntington, Colis P. | 23 |
| Hythe | 44 |
| Indian Bay | *53*,85,*88* |
| Indians | 7 |
| Industrial Rwys. | 85-102 |
| Insects | 7 |
| Intercolonial | 29,31 |
| International Falls | 47 |
| Jasper | 35 |
| Jiggers | 58 |
| Jubilee Locos | *18* |
| Kamloops | 29,*35* |
| Kaslo & Slocan | 47 |
| Kenora | *19* |
| Keremeos | 47 |
| Kerensky | 43 |
| Kettle Valley Rwy. | 11 |
| Kicking Horse Pass | 14 |
| Kimberley | 99 |
| Kingsgate | 10 |
| Kitimat | 100 |
| Klondike | 76,80,*84* |
| Kootenay & Elk | 10 |
| Kootenay Central | 11 |
| Kootenay Landing | 11 |
| Kootenays | 10,*20*,*21* |
| Lac La Biche | 43 |
| Ladysmith | 23,*54*,60,95,*97* |
| Lake Louise | 9 |
| Lake Manitoba Rwy. | 31 |
| Lake Superior | 10 |
| Langley | 68,71 |
| Lasers | 9 |
| Lethbridge | *6*,10,11,*20* |
| Lillooet | 61 |
| Linear Induction | 115-117 |
| Locomotive Cabs | 30,*45*,*63* |
| Speed | 18,46 |
| Strength | 9,14,30 |
| Washing | 63 |
| Logging | 27,89-98 |
| London, England | 67,103 |
| Long Beach | 23 |
| Louise Bridge | *22* |
| Lulu Island | 67,69 |
| Lynn Lake | 29 |
| MacDonald, John A. | 23 |

| | | | | | | | |
|---|---|---|---|---|---|---|---|
| Mackenzie & Mann | 29 | Radio Control | 9,25,*37*,58,85,95,113 | Tumbler Ridge | *51*,57,65 | | |
| Mackenzie River | 42 | Rapid Transit | *55,56*,103-108 | Tunnels | 2,9,11,14,15,16,30,31,51,77, | | |
| MacLeod | 11 | Red River | 22,31 | | 109,115,117 | | |
| Macmillan Bloedel | 89,*90* | Revelstoke | 14,17 | Union Pacific | 10 | | |
| McArthur Co. | *34*,43 | Richmond | *69*,116 | Unit Trains | 9,11,*21,40*,57 | | |
| McCauley Door | 107 | Ridley Island | *65* | Unloading | *39,64,65,74*,82,*88,94,96,97,101* | | |
| McLennan | 43,*50* | Riel, Louis | 11 | U.S. Army | 77 | | |
| Maple Ridge | 90 | Riverboats | *80,84* | U.T.D.C. | 115 | | |
| Microwave | 58 | Robbery | 7 | Vancouver | 8,9,17,*22*,30,37,47,*53,56,* | | |
| Midland Rwy. | 47 | Roberts Bank | 11,21,40,57,*65* | | 67,77,*103-105*,115-117 | | |
| Midway | 11 | Rocanville | 99 | Vancouver Island | 11,23-29,*35,41,54,* | | |
| Milwaukee Road | 10 | Rogers, A.B. | 10,11 | | *69*,89-98 | | |
| Miner, Bill | 7 | Rogers Pass | 2,9,11,14,15,16,*21* | Vancouver Wharves | *102* | | |
| Minerals | 47,77,*83*,99 | Roma Junction | 42 | Van Horne, Wm. | 10,11 | | |
| Minnesota & Manitoba | 31 | Rotary Dumpers | *64,65* | Vedder Mountain | *71* | | |
| Mission | 7,11 | Rotary Plows | *20* | Vernon | 29 | | |
| Moncton | 29 | Royal Train | 17 | Vernon, Van. Is. | 91 | | |
| Moose | 58,85 | Rule of Road | 105 | Via Rail | 2,9,11,*19*,24,30,*37* | | |
| Moose Jaw | 10 | Ruskin | 68 | Victoria | 23,*41*,47,67,103 | | |
| Morden | 31,47 | St. Boniface | 85,*86,87*,88 | Wabamun | *41* | | |
| Mountain Hazards | 7,14,15,58,*62* | St. John, N.D. | 47 | War | 29,45,57,77 | | |
| Muskeg | 7,*46* | St. Paul & Pacific | 10,11 | Waskada | 31 | | |
| Nanaimo | 23,60,99 | Sask. Midland | 31 | Waterways | 42,46 | | |
| Nanaimo Lakes | 54,95,*98* | Sask. North Western | 31 | Wellington Colliery | 23 | | |
| Nanoose Bay | 23 | Satellites | 9 | Western Extension Rwy. | 31 | | |
| Narrow Gauge | 47,77 | Schnellbahn | 109 | Whistler | 58 | | |
| National Transcontinental | 29,31 | Seaton Lake | 60-*62* | White Horse | 77,*82-84* | | |
| Nelson | 11,*20*,47,*107* | Seattle | 47 | White Pass & Yukon | *52*,76-84 | | |
| Nelson Valley Rwy. | 31 | Selkirk | *14,17*,22 | White Rock | 47 | | |
| New Westminster | 31,47,*48,51*,67,*70,* | Shay | *92* | Winnipeg | 9,10,11,17,*22*,29,31,47,85,103 | | |
| | 71,*75*,115 | Shuswap & Okanagan | 11 | Winter | 7,45,77,133 | | |
| Nimpkish | 91 | Siemens-Duwag | 109,*111*,113,*114* | | see also Snow | | |
| North Vancouver | 57,*61,64*,67,*101* | Skagway | 77-79,*83* | Woss | 91,93 | | |
| Northern Alberta Rwys. | 29,31,42-46,*50* | Slugs | *63* | Yale | 11 | | |
| Northern Extension Rwy. | 31 | Smelting | 100 | Yellowhead | 10,11,29,30 | | |
| Northern Pacific | 10,11,31 | Smith, Donald | 10 | Yorkton | 11 | | |
| see also BNR | | Snow | 15,20,29,*42*,58,*104* | | | | |
| Observation Coaches | 9,*19,60,79*,105 | Solid Trains | 9 | | | | |
| Oil | 35,43,45,47,67,77,103 | Soo Line | 10,11 | | | | |
| Okanagan | 29 | Speeders | *98* | | | | |
| Ontario & Rainy Lake Rwy. | 31 | Squamish | 57-61 | | | | |
| Oregon Electric | 111 | Stanford, L. | 23 | | | | |
| Pacific Elevators | *53* | Stations | 7,*17,18*,25,*37,50,55,56*,67,*68,* | | | | |
| Pacific Great Eastern — see BCR | | | 69,*79,84*,85,109,115,*117* | | | | |
| Parksville | 24 | Stave Falls | 68 | | | | |
| Passenger Trains | 9,*17-19*,30,57,58,60, | Steam Donkeys | 89 | | | | |
| | 61,67,77,80 | Steel | 29 | | | | |
| Peace River | 42,*45* | Stephen, George | 10,11 | | | | |
| Pembina Branch Rwy. | 43 | Stoney Creek | *21* | | | | |
| Penticton | 11 | Streetcars — see Rapid Transit | | | | | |
| Piggyback | *15* | Sulphur | 9,10,30,47,99,102 | | | | |
| Pine Point | 42,43 | Supercontinental | 30,*36* | | | | |
| Pioneer | 99 | Swan Landing | 42 | | | | |
| Pioneer Grain | 100,*101* | Swift Current | 9 | | | | |
| Port Alberni | 9,23,*26* | Switchbacks | 77 | | | | |
| Port Arthur | 31,101 | Tancrede, T. | 77 | | | | |
| Port Moody | 11 | Tank Cars | 67,77,*88,102* | | | | |
| Portage La Prairie | 11,31,47 | The Pas | 31,*34* | | | | |
| Potash | 9,10,30,*39*,47,99,*102* | Thunder Bay | 9,11,14,17,*18,39* | | | | |
| Prairie Locos | 60 | Tod Inlet | *69* | | | | |
| Preservation | 8,*35,54,81,92*,99 | Tofield | *36* | | | | |
| Presidents Conference Cars | *108*,109,115 | Track | 30,*38*,39,109,113,118 | | | | |
| Prince George | 57 | Trackmobile | *90* | | | | |
| Prince Rupert | 29,31,57 | Trail | 100 | | | | |
| Private Cars | 99,*102* | Trailers | *15*,23 | | | | |
| Qualicum Beach | *25* | Train Size | 9,14,30 | | | | |
| Qu'Appelle | 31 | Trapp | *51,74* | | | | |
| Quesnel | 57 | Trevithick, R. | 99 | | | | |

# SELECTED BIBLIOGRAPHY

Berton, Pierre, *The National Dream* (CPR to 1881), Toronto: McClelland & Stewart, 1970.

Berton, Pierre, *The Last Spike* (CPR 1881-85), Toronto: McClelland & Stewart, 1971.

Burrows, Roger, *Railway Mileposts,* Vol. 1 (CPR Mainline in B.C.) and Vol. 2 (Southern B.C. Routes), N. Vancouver: Milepost, 1981 and 1984.

Cohen, Stan, *White Pass & Yukon Route,* Missoula: Pictorial, 1980.

Ewart, Henry, *Story of the BC Electric,* N. Vancouver: Whitecap, 1986.

Hatcher, Colin K., *Stampede City Streetcars,* Montreal: Railfare, 1975.

Hatcher, C.K. and Schwartzkopf, T., *Edmonton's Electric Transit,* Toronto: Railfare, 1983.

Hearn, G. and Wilkie, D., *The Cordwood Limited* (Victoria & Sidney Rwy.), Victoria: BC Railway Historical Association, 1976.

Lamb, W. Kaye, *History of the Canadian Pacific,* New York: Macmillan, 1977.

Lavallee, Omer, *Narrow Gauge Railways of Canada,* Montreal: Railfare, 1972.

Lavallee, Omer, *Van Horne's Road*, Montreal: Railfare, 1974.

Leggett, Robt. F., *Railways of Canada*, Vancouver: Douglas & McIntyre, 1973.

Letourneau, Rodger, "GWWD: Manitoba's Uncommon Carrier", *Railfan & Railroad* magazine, May 1981, pp. 50-57.

Liddell, Ken, *I'll Take The Train,* Saskatoon: Western Producer, 1977.

Martin, J. Edward, *Railway Stations of Western Canada,* White Rock: Studio E. 1980.

Middleton, William D., *The Interurban Era,* Milwaukee: Kalmbach, 1961.

Middleton, William D., *Time of the Trolley,* Milwaukee: Kalmbach, 1967.

Moore, George A., "Manitoba's Railways", *Canadian Rail* No. 282, July 1975 and No. 285, October 1975.

Ramsey, Bruce, *PGE: Railway To The North,* Vancouver: Mitchell, 1962.

Regehr, T.D., *The Canadian Northern Railway,* Toronto: Macmillan, 1976.

Sanford, Barrie, *McCulloch's Wonder* (Kettle Valley Rwy.), Vancouver: Whitecap, 1977.

Sanford, Barrie, *Pictorial History of Railroading in British Columbia,* N. Vancouver: Whitecap, 1981.

Stevens, G.R., *History of the Canadian National Railways,* New York: Macmillan, 1973.

Todd, John, "Jim Hill's Canadian Railway", *Canadian Rail* No. 283, August 1975.

Turner, Robert D., *Railroaders: Recollections of the Steam Era in British Columbia,* Victoria: Provincial Archives, 1981.

Turner, Robert D., *Vancouver Island Railroads,* San Marino: Golden West, 1973.

Wood, Charles R., *Lines West* (Great Northern Rwy.), New York: Bonanza, 1967.


**For Data On Locomotives**

Bytown Railway Society, *Trackside Guide,* Ottawa: Bytown, 1984 etc.

Clegg, A. and Corley, R., *Canadian National Steam Power,* Montreal: Trains and Trolleys, 1969.

Hind, Patrick O., *Pacific Great Eastern Steam Locomotives,* Victoria: BC Railway Historical Association, 1984.

Lavallee, Omer, *Canadian Pacific Steam*, Toronto: Railfare, 1985.

Lewis, D.C., *Rail Canada* (Diesel Paint Schemes) Vol. 1 (CNR), Vol. 2 (PGE, NAR etc.), Vol. 3 (CPR), Vol. 4 (Via), Vancouver: Launchpad, 1983.

*About the Author...*

*J.Edward Martin's interest in railways has sent him notebook and camera in hand from coast to coast, and to many countries of western Europe. He was a founding member of the Forest City Railway Society in London, Ontario, where before moving West in the early 1970s he contributed lectures and written articles on railway subjects. In 1980, his first book, **Railway Stations of Western Canada** explored the history and construction of that fascinating segment of railroad lore and its success encouraged the preparation of this present volume.*

*Educated in London, Toronto and Ottawa, the author obtained degrees in Art History and Canadian Studies. For several years he lectured at the university level.*

A long train of empty grain cars snakes slowly up the Fraser Canyon at Cisco, heading back to the prairies via CN Rail.